THE CHURCH'S
MISSION to
THE GENTILES

ACTS OF THE APOSTLES,
EPISTLES OF PAUL

THE CHURCH'S
MISSION to
THE GENTILES

ACTS OF THE APOSTLES, EPISTLES OF PAUL

Naymond H. Keathley

SMYTH&HELWYS
PUBLISHING, INCORPORATED MACON, GEORGIA

ISBN 1-57312-185-1
The Church's Mission to the Gentiles
Acts of the Apostles, Epistles of Paul

Naymond H. Keathley

Copyright © 1999
Smyth & Helwys Publishing, Inc.
6316 Peake Road
Macon, Georgia 31210-3960
1-800-747-3016

Library of Congress Cataloging-in-Publication Data

Keathley, Naymond H.
        The church's mission to the Gentiles:
        Acts of the Apostles, Epistles of Paul/
        Naymond H. Keathley.
        p.   cm.
        Includes bibliographical references (p.).
        ISBN 1-57312-185-1   (alk. paper)
        1. Bible. N.T. Acts—Criticism, interpretation, etc.
        2. Bible. N.T. Epistles of Paul—Criticism,
        interpretation, etc. 3. Church history—Primitive
        and early church, ca. 30–600. I. Title.
        BS2617.5.K43 1999
        227'.06—dc21   98-50648
                                                    CIP

Contents

Acknowledgments

No written work emerges out of a vacuum. People and ideas and experiences always contribute to the product that finally appears in printed form. Certainly, that has been the case for me, for my associations with various groups and individuals have proven to be formidable, not only for my ideas in particular, but also for my life in general. Thus I would like to acknowledge my indebtedness and to express my profound appreciation to and for the following:

- My New Testament teachers, William E. Hull, Frank Stagg, Harold S. Songer, and Wayne E. Ward, who instilled in me a love and reverence for the biblical text and guided me with their own insights and understandings of it

- Baylor University, which has provided me with a felicitous context in which to fulfill my Christian vocation, colleagues from whom I continue to learn, and students who challenge and stimulate my thinking

- My family, whose love and support I feel daily: Carolyn, Kristen, Craig and Beth, Kevin and Jana, Claire and Rachel

ACTS OF THE APOSTLES

Introduction
The Book of Acts

A cts is unique. To be sure, one could accurately claim that
the New Testament contains twenty-seven unique
books. Each makes its own individual and singularly significant contribution to understanding the meaning of the Christ
event. The four Gospels are not mere repetitions of the same
story. Though they deal with the same subject matter, each
has its own distinctive approach in presenting a narrative
account about Jesus. Likewise, the Epistles, although they all
conform to a basic literary pattern, are unique in that they
are addressed to distinctively different groups and individuals
and deal with a variety of different issues.

Acts, though, is unique in another way. It is the only book
of its kind within the New Testament. If one of the Gospels
were lost, we would still have three others. If one of the
Epistles were missing, twenty others would remain. But Acts
is unparalleled. It alone recounts the history of the early
church. If we did not have it, we would know very little about
the beginnings of Christianity. Certainly, other writers on
occasion allude to isolated historical events or convey historical information, but Acts is the only document that sets out
to record a history of the first three decades of the Christian
movement.

The traditional title of the book, "The Acts of the
Apostles," is also unique. Probably none of the original New
Testament documents had titles. The community for which
each was written knew what the document was and what it

contained. As long as it was the only document the community possessed, a title was unnecessary. When these early churches began to share copies of their documents with each other, however, titles written on the outside of the individual scrolls became a necessity so that each document could be identified even when it was closed (rolled up). In this process various titles were given to this document: "Acts of All the Apostles," "Acts of the Apostles," and simply "Acts."

As a rule, the titles added to other New Testament books are appropriate; they are Gospels, Epistles, and an Apocalypse. The title for this book is unique, though, in that it is somewhat misleading. In the ancient world writers used the term "Acts" as a title for literature that described the exploits of famous characters such as Hercules or Alexander the Great. At the end of the second century one of the earliest sources to refer to this document, the Muratorian canon, called it "The Acts of All the Apostles." Surely this title is inappropriate, for the contents do not record the activities of *all* the apostles. The author seems to use the term "apostle" almost exclusively to describe the Twelve, the disciples of Jesus. All twelve names are listed in the first chapter of the book, but afterwards only three are mentioned again. In no way, then, is this "The Acts of *All* the Apostles." Furthermore, the two main characters of Acts are Peter, the leader of the Twelve, and Paul who was never a part of this group the author calls apostles. Obviously, then, even the shorter traditional title "Acts of the Apostles" does not aptly describe what the author intends to convey.

Another unique feature of Acts is that it is a sequel to another volume, the Gospel of Luke. To be sure, some churches—Thessalonica and Corinth are examples—are listed as recipients of more than one letter from an author, but the letters are not seen as two parts of a whole. Each letter is an independent document. Luke and Acts, though, are two parts of one work. They share a common style and vocabulary. Unlike other New Testament documents, they begin with literary prefaces; and the opening words of Acts (1:1) mention that it was preceded by a first book. Both are dedicated to the same person, Theophilus. Acts is a continuation of the story that begins in the Third Gospel.

What is that story? Following the traditional style of ancient biography, it is a narrative of the life of Jesus and his immediate successors.[1] Specifically, this second volume traces the development of the early Christian church as a natural continuation of the account of the life and teachings of Jesus. Several emphases can be detected in the telling of the story. In Acts the community that had its origins in truest Judaism becomes a movement with universal significance. The little Jewish sect originally confined to Palestine stretches forth to include Gentiles living in the uttermost parts of the earth. Moreover, the narrative is dominated by the activities of two central characters, Peter and Paul. Yet, the story is not simply *about* them; it is not their story. Instead, it is about the unstoppable triumph of the gospel that they among others proclaimed.[2]

Finally, the traditions of the church have accorded Acts, coupled with Luke, one other claim to uniqueness within the Scriptures: a Gentile author. Actually, both Luke and Acts are anonymous; the two documents include no claims about authorship, and neither even mentions someone named "Luke." From late second century to the present, though, the dominant view has asserted that the two documents were written by Luke the beloved physician and traveling companion of Paul mentioned in Colossians 4:14, Philemon 24, and 2 Timothy 4:11.

Four times in recording his narrative (16:10-17; 20:5-15; 21:1-18; 27:1-28:16) the author abruptly changes from third-person personal pronouns (he, him, they, them) to the first-person plural forms (we, us). Readers through the ages have concluded, then, that the author must have been with Paul on the occasions described by the so-called "we" passages. As far as we can tell from available documents, the second-century Irenaeus was the first to suggest that this traveling companion and author was Luke,[3] and most readers since that time have been comfortable with that conclusion.

Attempts by scholars either to prove or to disprove Lukan authorship on the basis of writing style and vocabulary have been inconclusive, but several factors are problematic for accepting the traditional view. Most significant, for example, is the absence of any reference in Acts to the letters of Paul. Was the author unaware of them? Could a close traveling companion of Paul not have known about them? If he was familiar with them, why did he not mention this significant aspect of Paul's mission effort?

Furthermore, the "collection" among the Gentile churches for the church in Jerusalem was a major effort for Paul that occupied his thoughts as he wrote his three longest letters (see Rom 15; 1 Cor 16; 2 Cor 8–9). Yet, Acts has hardly a hint about this strategic endeavor! Did the author not know about it, or did he omit an account of the collection on purpose?[4] Other themes in Paul's thought, such as justification by faith, also receive scant reference in Acts, and impressions of Paul derived from the Epistles do not always coincide with those gained from the narrative in Acts.

Perhaps the more expedient alternative is to affirm the anonymity of Luke-Acts. With the evidence now available, the identity of the author cannot be firmly established. Is there any evidence, though, that suggests the author was indeed a Gentile? Perhaps so. His facile use of the Greek language, among the best in the New Testament, and his knowledge of Greek rhetoric, literature, and thought have convinced many of his Gentile origins. He certainly emphasized the inclusiveness of Christianity, that Jesus is Savior for all people and not just the Jews alone. In Acts one of his major concerns was to show the triumph of Gentile Christianity. Consequently, it seems reasonable to assume that he himself was of Gentile origin.

Yet, he also had an extensive familiarity with the Old Testament, specifically, the Greek version of the Hebrew scriptures. Likely, then, he was a Gentile who came to Christianity though Judaism, either as a convert or as one attracted to Judaism for quite some time before he became a Christian.[5] Although we cannot be certain about his identity, we will use the traditional name Luke in our study as a convenient way of referring to him.

Luke was not the first to write a Gospel (Luke 1:1-4), but he was the first to write a history of Christianity. Although other Christian writers before him apparently did not consider the writing of such a volume to be either necessary or desirable, Luke plowed new ground by including this material in his "account of the events that have been fulfilled among us." Especially interesting is his use of the phrase "among us." He admitted in this preface that he was not an eyewitness to Jesus. What did he mean, then, by referring to events "that have been fulfilled among us"? Did they not include those events collectively experienced by him and his readers in the first century church?

Because of his use of "among us," we can conclude that his introduction stated at the beginning of the Gospel is actually a preface to *both* volumes. As indicated earlier, Luke saw that the activities of the early church were indeed a continuation of the story that had begun in Jesus. We know, though, from our study of his Gospel[6] that Luke did not simply record facts, nor did he attempt to record everything he knew about Jesus. Rather he carefully selected, arranged, and edited the stories handed down to him by those who were "eyewitnesses and servants of the word" in order to craft his own "portrait" of Jesus. By his choice and adaptation of these stories, Luke gave to his readers his understanding, his interpretation, of the meaning of Jesus' life. Since Acts continues the story begun in the Gospel, we should probably assume that the selectivity and interpretative skills that the author applied in the first volume were utilized in the second also.

Luke's selectivity is quite apparent to the reader who compares the incidents recorded in the Third Gospel with those found in the other three. At times this Gospel includes the only account of a particular event, while frequently the author has related a story that is shared with one, two, or even all three of the other Gospels. In no way has he duplicated every incident found in the others; they, too, have preserved materials unique to them.

When we study Acts, however, we do not have another biblical book similar to Acts with which we can compare it. Thus we sometimes overlook the fact that the author employed in this sequel the same investigative and interpretative skills characteristic of the first. He obviously has not tried to tell us everything about the early church. Since Acts contains twenty-eight chapters and covers a period of more than thirty years, we might initially think that each chapter covers roughly one year in the history of the church. But Acts 2 is devoted to the events of only one *day*, while Acts 19 covers the three *years* Paul spent in Ephesus. As a matter of fact, the first third of Acts (chaps. 1–9) spans the events of the first three years of the church, while the last two-thirds covers a period of more than twenty-five years! The history is a disproportionate one; it is highly selective.

Was the author arbitrary in his choice of materials, or was there a purpose that guided his selections? Returning to his first preface (Luke 1:1-4), we find a hint of his intent: Luke wanted his readers to have an orderly account that would enable them to know the truth about what had happened among them. What was that truth? What was the author's intention? What was his purpose?[7]

Over the years, as one can easily imagine, a variety of proposals have been offered to explain Luke's intention, but I have been intrigued in particular by a comment in Raymond Brown's recent New Testament introduction. Contrary to one theory that has often been proposed, he suggests that Luke was not writing an apologetic, a defense of Christianity for those outside the movement. Rather, Luke was concerned to help the insiders with their own self-understanding; his purpose was "to explain the status quo."[8] Expanding upon this idea, I think we can explore this status quo from two perspectives, historical and theological.

Historical Agenda

Writing toward the end of the first century, Luke wanted his readers to understand not only their origins, but also the process by which they had become who they were. Specifically, the church at the time of Luke was predominantly Gentile. Yet, it had begun as a movement within Judaism. Jesus and his immediate followers were Jews, and in the first two to three years after his resurrection, virtually all of those who were part of the church were of Jewish ancestry. How did a movement that began as what could perhaps be described as a reform movement within Judaism become one in which Jews were greatly outnumbered by Gentiles? How did a church that began on Palestinian soil become an organization spread throughout the Roman empire?

Foreshadowings of this agenda are evident in the Gospel. That the story recorded here stresses the inclusiveness of Jesus is a commonplace. More is found about lepers, tax collectors, Samaritans, and women in this account than in any other. If Jesus reached out to these on the lowest rungs on the ladder of Palestinian society, was he not indeed the Savior of all people, including the Gentiles? The very first incident in Luke's arrangement of Jesus' public ministry gives a glimpse of what is to come: Jesus was rejected by his own people in Nazareth (Luke 4:14-30), but this setback did not defeat his ministry. Likewise, Luke was aware, Jesus' early followers experienced rejection when they reached out to their fellow Jews, but the Christian movement was not defeated. They experienced triumph as they turned to the receptive Gentiles. This is the part of the story contained in the second book.

Logically, three major focal points emerge in Luke's presentation of the chronology of the post-resurrection community. The first concentrates on the beginnings when Christianity was primarily a Jewish movement centered in and effectively limited to Jerusalem (Acts 1:1–6:7). Second and crucial to the church's self-understanding, the middle section describes in stages the transition from a thoroughly Jewish group to one that includes Gentiles (6:8–15:35). Finally, the third and major portion of the book emphasizes the ascendancy of Gentile Christianity (15:36–28:31). Earlier I noted that the two major characters in the book are Peter and Paul. According to this analysis of the book, Peter is featured in the first section; both Peter and Paul are key figures in the second; and Paul totally dominates the third.

Another aspect of the historical status quo that Luke clarified for his readers was the relationship of the church to the state. Before Luke wrote, the Christians had undergone their first official persecution instigated by the Roman government (AD 64). Moreover, Palestinian Jews, from whom the church had its origins, had revolted and fought a full scale war against the Romans in 66–70. In the light of these events Christians were often seen by their detractors as subversives opposed to the imperial government.

Luke, however, wrote to remind his readers that their origins were politically innocent and that they were not seditious revolutionaries. Every time in Acts that Christians are brought before Roman officials, these followers of Jesus are never found guilty. Contrary to earlier popular opinion, these accounts did not offer an apology to outsiders to emphasize that the church was not in conflict with Rome. Instead, as Brown suggests, Luke wrote for insiders who were often subjected to malicious accusations to assure them that their origins and their past history did not put them at odds with Rome.[9]

Theological Agenda

Although frequently identified as the church's first historian, Luke was nonetheless a first-rate theologian. When he recorded history, he was not concerned simply to give a chronological account of a sequence of events. He was concerned about the *meaning* of those events. In all the history he recited, he saw God at work.

Specifically, Luke was a theologian whose emphasis was salvation history, a history he divided into three epochs.[10] God first revealed himself redemptively in the era of the law and the prophets, that is, the period covered in the Old Testament. In turn, this epoch was succeeded by the era of the gospel, the redemptive work God accomplished in Jesus. Finally, God was at work in Luke's own era, the period of the church. In other words, this last epoch was not an afterthought. It was not an accident. It was just as much a part of God's plan for salvation as the other two.

Luke's two volumes concentrate on these last two epochs, the period of Jesus and the period of the church. That the two are intricately bound up together, that they are two parts of one story, Luke indicated in the first verse of the second volume. Here he noted that his first book dealt with all Jesus *began* to do and teach, implying that this second book describes what Jesus *continues* to do and teach though his successors. Luke did not separate the work of Christ from the work of those described in Acts; they were two parts of one grand plan of salvation.

For the Gentile church, this concept was essential for their self-understanding. The sweep of salvation intended by God from the foundation of the world included *them*. They were a part of God's divine plan for the ages.

For Luke, then, the story he recorded in Acts was of paramount importance for understanding God. God who had delivered the Israelites in the Exodus was the same God who worked redemptively in Jesus Christ. But he was also the God who was bringing about the salvation of the Gentiles. For the story of God's redemptive purpose to be complete, Luke found it essential to tell the story of the church's mission to the Gentiles.

Notes

[1]Charles H. Talbert, *Reading Luke: A Literary and Theological Commentary on the Third Gospel* (New York: Crossroad, 1982) 2-3.

[2]Frank Stagg, *The Book of Acts: The Early Struggle for an Unhindered Gospel* (Nashville: Broadman, 1955) 12-17.

[3]For a probable explanation of how Irenaeus arrived at this conclusion, see John B. Polhill, *Acts*, The New American Commentary, vol. 26 (Nashville: Broadman, 1992) 25.

[4]See pp. 79-80.

[5]Raymond E. Brown, *An Introduction to the New Testament*, The Anchor Bible Reference Library (New York: Doubleday, 1997) 268.

[6]Linda McKinnish Bridges, *The Church's Portraits of Jesus* (Macon GA: Smyth & Helwys, 1997) 63-82.

[7]Obviously, we can never completely and precisely determine the intentions of others, particularly of those who lived centuries ago. We can assess what they have done, though, and we often conclude that these results fulfilled original intentions. Comments about intentionality, therefore, actually reveal how we the readers understand the texts and what we perceive to be the author's purpose.

[8]Brown, 271-72.

[9]Ibid.

[10]Generally, every serious study of Luke since the middle of the twentieth century has been influenced by the pioneering work of Hans Conzelmann who proposed this understanding of Luke in his *The Theology of St Luke*, trans. Geoffrey Buswell (New York: Harper & Row, 1961).

Prelude to the Gentile Mission
(Acts 1:1–6:7)

This record of the earliest period of the church was not an eyewitness account. Whether or not the author was a traveling companion of Paul, this material, like the whole of the Third Gospel, was dependent upon written and oral traditions handed down to the author by those who had preceded him in the faith. Such a fact does not make the text less reliable, but it does explain the nature of the history that is recorded. The material is episodic; the author has not produced a flowing day-by-day, week-by-week, or even month-by-month chronicle of the activities of these early followers of Jesus. He has written skillfully, however, with such smooth transitions that readers are not generally aware of gaps in time between some of the recorded incidents. With just a couple of exceptions that we will examine later in this chapter, the impression that emerges of the church in this period is rather idealized. Although there was some opposition from without, the church was tranquil within; everyone was in harmony with each other (2:44; 4:32; 6:7).

Although most of the book concentrates on the expansion of Christianity beyond the limits of Judaism, the Jerusalem church played a pivotal role in this scenario. It was the "mother" church. Here the story began. From here the story developed. The pivotal conference that dealt with the acceptance of Gentiles assembled here (ch. 15), and later, though Paul concentrated his ministry elsewhere, he returned at significant junctures to report to this church in this city (18:22; 21:15ff.) Appropriately, then, in the beginning of his account Luke concentrated on the early developments in this congregation. Four ideas give shape to this section: continuity, growth, opposition from without, and discord from within.

Continuity

Various incidents, themes, and terms reminding the reader that the story in Acts is a continuation of the story found in the Gospel of Luke are found throughout this section; indeed, some are found throughout the whole book. Yet, in the first chapter Luke emphasizes this continuity. In the first verse, for example, he refers to his first book, the Gospel of Luke, linking the story in the present volume with what he has written in the former. As in the Gospel, moreover, Luke dedicates the volume to the same person, Theophilus. Not mentioned outside these two books in the New Testament, this name, derived from Greek words meaning "one who loves God," may refer to an actual person, or it could be a pseudonym for any Christian reader. Finally, Luke implies that what he is describing in this volume is a continuation of "all that Jesus did and taught." This is no new narrative, but a second installment of the one begun in the Gospel.

The first incident recorded in the narrative is the ascension (1:6-11). It is precisely the same incident with which Luke ends the Gospel. All of us familiar with television movies that extend to two nights or more recognize the device Luke has used here. The second night of our modern telecast usually shows scenes from the night before, particularly the scene with which the previous presentation ended. In this way the two nights' presentations are seamed together: the incident that closes the first becomes the opening scene in the second. Luke has bound his two volumes together in the same way by his dual references to the ascension. Interesting is the fact that Luke alone tells of this final earthly experience of Jesus, and he tells it twice!

The account in Acts is not merely rote repetition of what has already been stated. In fact, new information is added, such as the indication that the ascension took place forty days after the resurrection (1:3). Especially significant, though, are the words of Jesus found in Acts and not in the Gospel (1:8). Jesus commissioned the disciples to be witnesses in Jerusalem, in Judea and Samaria,[1] and to the ends of the earth. Although Luke's purpose is not simply to describe the geographical expansion of Christianity,[2] this verse does set the geographical agenda that Luke will follow as he tells the rest of the story in Acts.

After Jesus ascended into heaven, the apostles returned to the upper room in Jerusalem where they had been staying. Here (1:13) the reader finds a list of the Twelve, with the exception of Judas, corresponding to that found in Luke 6:14-16. Again connecting the two books, Luke mentions that the core of the community of believers includes the same personalities that formed the band of Jesus' closest associates in the Gospel. Now in Acts they are gathered with Mary, Jesus' brothers, and some unnamed women (1:14). Just as the Gospel of Luke emphasizes Jesus' encounters with women more than the other three, so now in his second volume women continue in their role as followers of Jesus.

One final development in chapter 1 that connects the present story with the one that preceded it is the selection of Matthias to take the place of Judas (1:15-26). Here Luke ties up one of the loose ends of his Gospel, which does not mention the death of Judas, by recording the details of that story. Three features of the account should be noted.

First, after the resurrection Peter emerged as the leader, the spokesman for the band of followers, just as he had been during the ministry of Jesus. In the Passion Narrative, Jesus, knowing that Peter would deny him, admonished him: "When once you have turned back, strengthen your brothers" (Luke 22:31-32). Here, in assuming the role of leadership, Peter did just that!

Second, the mention of the Twelve does more to stress continuity with the past than it does to set the agenda for the story to follow. Ironically, nine of the Twelve (including Matthias) will not be mentioned again in Acts; others, not they, will provide the impetus for the expansion of Christianity among the Gentiles.

Finally, embedded in the narrative are clues about Luke's understanding and use of the term "apostle": the one added to the other apostles was one who had been with Jesus from the beginning (22:21), who was a witness to the resurrection (v. 22), and who was finally chosen by God (v. 24). Perhaps these qualifications explain Luke's reluctance to call Paul an apostle, for the latter was not one who had been with Jesus from the start.[3]

Growth

Overall, Acts describes the phenomenal growth and spread of Christianity during its first three decades. Chapter 2, however, offers a foretaste of what is to come by relating the story of Pentecost, one day in the life of the church—a day when membership swelled from about 120 (1:15) to more than 3,000 (2:41)!

Pentecost, a harvest celebration that had come to be associated with the giving of the covenant to the Israelites at Sinai, occurred fifty days after Passover. One of the great pilgrim feasts of the Jews, this occasion brought celebrants to Jerusalem from all over the Greco-Roman world. Because of its proximity in time to Passover, the greatest of the festivals, I imagine that Jews coming from great distances for their perhaps once-in-a-lifetime visit to Jerusalem extended their stays from Passover to Pentecost to include this second festive occasion. At any rate, the city on this day was filled with Jews and proselytes, or Gentiles who had converted to Judaism, from all over the Roman empire (2:9-11).

Suddenly, the Holy Spirit who had been promised by the resurrected Jesus (1:5) became a powerful reality for the assembled believers. Here, to describe an incredible spiritual, reality Luke uses powerful physical images of sound (2:2) and sight (2:3); and he indicates that they were given the ability to speak in "other tongues."

The exact nature of this experience has long been debated. Was it ecstatic utterance similar to what was later experienced in Corinth? Or were they miraculously given the ability to speak in other languages? The observation by some that the people were drunk (v. 13) seems to link the phenomenon with ecstatic speech; yet, unlike the experience in Corinth, the point here is that the tongues were understood. By the same token, if they were speaking other languages, why would some think that they were drunk? Then, as now, drunkenness was not the typical explanation given for the behavior of one speaking a foreign language. A possible solution is that the believers uttered ecstatic speech that was then heard by each bystander either in her or his native language (v. 6) or as the babbling of intoxicated people. The difference in what was heard might be explained by the openness of the hearers to receiving a message from God.

Response to Jesus' ministry, after all, was characterized by ambiguity. When he spoke in parables, some learned from these analogies truths about the kingdom of God. Others simply heard the tales told by a clever storyteller with the result that they heard without understanding (Luke 8:10). For some, the miracles were evidence of the inbreaking of the kingdom of God (11:20); for others, the mighty deeds indicated that Jesus was empowered by the evil one (11:15). All were presented with the same story or the same miracle; their responses were dependent on their openness to God. Responses to the disciples at Pentecost, then, were similar to the responses of the people to Jesus during his ministry. Only those who were open to hear heard in their native languages.

Certainly the significance of the Pentecost experience for those early believers was not that they had ecstatic experiences, but that they were enabled to communicate the good news about Christ. A former colleague once remarked: "The Holy Spirit does not come to make one feel good; he comes to empower one for a task." Pentecost demonstrates this insight; the phenomenon occurred to equip the people for communication. Whether the tongues were a miracle of speaking, of hearing, or of both, the point of the experience was that people heard and responded to the gospel.

Again we can see striking similarities between Luke's Gospel and Acts. At the beginning of Jesus' ministry the Spirit descended upon him in bodily form at the baptism (Luke 3:22), led him into the wilderness where he was tempted (4:1), and filled him as he returned to Galilee (4:14) and preached his inaugural sermon (4:16-30). Likewise, at the beginning of Acts, the Spirit filled the believers (Acts 2:4), one of whom, Peter, then rose to preach his inaugural sermon (2:14-36). What Jesus had begun to do and teach (1:1) continued in the life of the early church enabled by the Spirit of God.

Peter's message on this day included both a backward look and a forward gaze. He began by noting that the phenomenon observed by the bystanders was a fulfillment of Old Testament prophecy. In recording this sermon, Luke again emphasizes the continuity between the past and the present. This activity of the church is no afterthought in the mind of God; the quotations from the prophets demonstrate that he has always intended this era of the church.

Furthermore, Peter gave a hint of what was to be expected in the future: the promise was not only for the Jews who responded in Jerusalem, but also for all who were far away, that is, everyone whom the Lord called to him (2:39). Though maybe even Peter was unaware of the full implication of this message, Luke in these words foreshadows the course he describes in the rest of his book: the promise of salvation is also for the Gentiles, those ultimately far off!

After indicating the response of 3,000 people to the proclamation by Peter, Luke concludes this section with a summary of life in the early Christian community (2:42-47). The believers shared their possessions to meet the needs of the community,[4] and they devoted themselves to the teachings of the apostles. Worship included fellowship in the homes, particularly the Lord's Supper (the probable meaning of the "breaking of bread"), and prayers in the temple. These first converts were still faithful, practicing Jews. They did not give up the practices of Judaism as they came to Christ, for they did not see themselves as professing a new religion. They were affirming that the religious hopes of their ancestors had been fulfilled in Jesus Christ.

Opposition from Without

During the first two months following the death and resurrection of Jesus, as depicted in the first two chapters of Acts, there was no sign of continued opposition by the governing authorities. Surprisingly, even when the apostles preached on the street corners of Jerusalem at Pentecost, no official negative response arose. Unfortunately, however, the tranquillity suggested in particular by the closing summary in chapter 2 was not long-lived. Conflict, which characterized the ministry of Jesus, emerges for the church in chapter 3.

One afternoon Peter and John, about to enter the temple at the routine hour of prayer, heard the plea for alms from a man who had been lame from birth lying at the entrance to the inner courts. Peter's response was not to toss coins but to give something more precious. Invoking the presence and power of Jesus by calling on his name, Peter raised up the man and commanded him to walk. When the beggar began leaping about, a crowd gathered; and Peter preached. Not by the power of Peter or John, he proclaimed, was this man enabled to walk, but by faith in the name, the person, of Jesus (3:16). Jesus, who had begun to heal during his public ministry, now continued this activity through his disciples.

With all the commotion, the religious authorities could not stand still. The priests, the captain of the temple, and the Sadducees arrested them, binding them over for a hearing before the Sanhedrin the next morning (4:1-3). Sadducees were the aristocratic religious party associated with the priesthood and the temple. They had considerable political clout because of their collaboration with the ruling Romans.

Interesting here is the parallel with the experience of Jesus in the Gospel. Although he had experienced opposition from the more numerous Pharisees practically from the beginning of his ministry in Galilee, he did not raise the ire of the priestly group until he invaded their territory by cleansing the temple (Luke 19:45-46). At that point they became involved in the opposition that finally led to his death. Preaching and teaching in the temple (20:1), Jesus incurred the wrath of the Sadducees; later, preaching and teaching in the temple, Peter and John were subjected to the same type of opposition. Like a skillful composer, Luke develops motifs, the echoes of which will reverberate again and again throughout his "composition." Here he reiterates his opening theme in Acts: the story of the church is a continuation of the story of Jesus! Then, picking up the key idea of chapter 2, growth, he indicates in 4:4 the positive response of those who heard the temple sermon: the number of believers swelled to 5,000.

Brought before the Sanhedrin, the high court of the Jews, Peter preached (Acts 4:8-12). In these early chapters in Acts it seems that whenever two or three were gathered together, Peter preached! Not able to deny the healing in the temple, but fearful of the spread of this unorthodox movement, the Jewish leaders released Peter and John unharmed after admonishing them not to speak anymore in the name of Jesus.

When enjoined to silence, the apostles declared that they could not keep from telling what they had seen and heard (4:20). True to their word, they continued to speak with boldness (4:31), and subsequently they suffered the consequences. The high priest and the Sadducees arrested them for the second time (5:17-18).

During the night, though, an angel miraculously delivered them from prison, and at daybreak the apostles returned once again to the temple to continue their teaching. When they were sought out and brought before the Sanhedrin this time, they met an infuriated audience bent on the death penalty, for the apostles had specifically violated the orders they had received at the previous hearing. At this point the apostles were delivered by the intercession of Gamaliel, one of the leading rabbis of that time. Basically his advice to the high court was that they should avoid a hasty judgment. If this movement was of human origin, it would fizzle out on its own; but if it was from God, nothing they might do would stop it (5:38-39). As a result, these leaders of the church were flogged and then released, only to resume their preaching of Jesus once again (5:42). The opposition was substantial, but it did not deter the proclamation of the gospel!

Discord from Within

Overall the picture of the church in this first section of Acts tends toward the idyllic. At first glance Luke's summary statements (2:42, 46-47; 4:32) give the impression that the fellowship of believers was characterized by peace, joy, and harmony. There was not a single disgruntled member in the whole group. Now at the end of this first section, Luke admits two exceptions to the harmonious picture he has described. Since the church is, after all, made up of human beings, one should not be surprised to find examples of human frailty within it.

Ananias and Sapphira

Background for the episode about Ananias and Sapphira (5:1-11) is found at the end of Acts 4. Incorporating another summary statement into his history (4:32-35), Luke picks up a theme he mentioned in a previous summary (2:44-45). When needs arose within the community, those early believers who had personal possessions and property sold them to share with the others who were in want. As a specific example, the author records the experience of Barnabas (4:36-37). Known by his deeds as a "son of encouragement," he sold a piece of property and laid the proceeds at the apostles' feet.

Although the reaction of the congregation is not mentioned, I imagine they were overwhelmed by Barnabas's gift. Though he was not seeking affirmation, he had, after all, presented the money in a public setting. Is it not likely that he received recognition and public appreciation for his generosity? Probably in this light we should understand the motivation behind the activity of Ananias and his wife Sapphira. Wanting the kind of attention Barnabas had received, they, too, sold a piece of property with the intention of sharing the proceeds with the church. For some reason, though, at the last minute they conspired to pretend that they were bringing the total sale price when, as a matter of fact, they were keeping a portion for themselves. Ananias first, and then Sapphira, told the same concocted story to the assembly. Somehow Peter perceived their lie; and when he confronted each of them with the truth, each fell dead.

For modern readers, this story is perplexing. The text does not indicate that Peter struck them dead. For that matter, it does not indicate that God did, although that is what we typically infer. Herein lies the problem: why did God strike them dead when others who lie, including ourselves, do not suffer the same consequences? Some interpreters suggest that they actually died of shock when, thinking that only they shared their secret, they were confronted publicly with their misdeed.[5]

Whatever the interpretation, the episode contributes to the narrative in two ways. First, it reiterates a theme found frequently in the Gospel about the perils of possessions. What a person owns or seeks to possess often stands between that one and God.[6] Second, it provides Luke with the opportunity to describe the paradoxical reaction of the people to the church. Those who observed the believers were so impressed with their high moral standards that they dared not join them (5:13), yet more than ever new converts were added to their number (5:14). In spite of the tendency of the general populace to hold the church in great esteem—yet at a distance— evidently the church experienced growth with the addition of those willing to commit themselves to Christ and to his weighty moral demands.

Hebrews and Hellenists

Whereas the first example of discord involved two people out of harmony with the rest of the church, the second concerned two groups within the church that were out of harmony with each other (6:1-7). Since all Christians at this time were Jews, both "Hebrews" and "Hellenists" refer to types of Jewish

Christians. Generally, interpreters identify the Hebrews as native Palestinian Jewish Christians who spoke Aramaic and the Hellenists as non-Palestinian Greek-speaking Jewish Christians. Neither group originated within Christianity; both came into the church from first-century Judaism. Native-born Jews from the Jerusalem area had a tendency to look down upon those raised anywhere other than Judea, particularly those born outside Palestine who grew up speaking Greek. When Jews from both groups became believers, the distrust of one for the other carried over into the church.

Picking up the idea of the church's characteristic sharing of goods, Luke in 6:1 indicates that controversy erupted between these two factions over the daily distribution. The Hellenists complained that their widows were being neglected. To resolve the difficulty, the Twelve suggested that the community select seven respected men to oversee this task of serving tables, thus freeing the apostles for prayer and "serving the word" (6:4).

The congregation reacted enthusiastically and selected the Seven (6:5-6). Although we cannot prove that all seven were Hellenists, this possibility seems likely since all had Greek names. If so, the choice demonstrated that the church was truly trying to preserve unity. The ones appointed to resolve the problem were chosen from among the group that had complained about their neglect.

Two factors in this narrative should not go unnoticed. First is the self-perception of the Twelve. They felt it was not right for them to neglect the word so they could wait on tables (6:2). Did they consider table service a menial task that was beneath their station? Had they forgotten Jesus' words in the upper room that the greater among them is the one who serves (Luke 22:27), or his teaching that one actually serves God by serving fellow human beings (11:29-37)? Their comment that they should "serve the word" is somewhat ironic. As we shall see later, two of the seven chosen to serve tables far excelled the Twelve in serving the word!

Second, this incident for Luke is somewhat transitional. It sets the stage for the next part of the story, the expansion of

Christianity beyond Judaism, by introducing us to two of the main characters in that development. Although all of the Seven are listed by name, only the first two, Stephen and Philip, play a role in the rest of the story. And, oh, what a role they play!

Notes

[1]Judea and Samaria were two adjoining geographical areas in Palestine, but they were combined by the Romans into one political jurisdiction ruled directly by Roman governors. Thus, this commission envisions a threefold geographical progression: city, province, and the world.

[2]Although it is not uncommon for interpreters to cite geographical expansion as the major purpose of Acts, the text omits too much material for this to be correct. How Christianity spread to Damascus, for example, is not described; and although the book does tell how Paul got to Rome, it does not tell how the gospel got there. A thriving church was active in Rome long before Paul arrived.

[3]"Apostle" technically means "one who is sent." Convinced that he was called by God to be sent to the Gentiles, Paul habitually used this term for himself. Only in Acts 14:4, 14, however, does Luke use this term for Paul, perhaps here meaning simply "one sent out" by the church at Antioch. Otherwise, Luke reserved the word only for those with these three qualifications.

[4]That this practice was not communal ownership of goods is indicated by the verb tenses in v. 45 that indicate a recurring practice. As needs arose within the community, those with property and goods sold what they had and apportioned the proceeds accordingly. Questions asked of Ananias in Acts 5:4 further indicate that early Christians were not required to sell all their possessions upon entrance into the community; rather the sale of personal property was an individual response made by one who wished to meet the needs of others.

[5]See, for example, Frank Stagg, *The Book of Acts: The Early Struggle for an Unhindered Gospel* (Nashville: Broadman, 1955) 83.

[6]Luke 12:13-21, for example, deals with the problem of covetousness.

Transition to the Gentile Mission
(6:8–15:35)

Jesus' departing words to the apostles indicated that after empowerment by the Spirit they would be witnesses in Jerusalem, Judea and Samaria, and finally throughout the world (Acts 1:8). Up until this point in the story, though, they have been content to be witnesses in Jerusalem alone. They have not really ventured outside the city. In this second phase of the church's story, however, we find the transition to the full realization of Jesus' commission. The spread of the gospel progresses from Jerusalem through the province of Judea-Samaria to territories far beyond Palestine.

This section also provides another, more significant type of transition: from a totally Jewish church to one that includes Gentiles. Just as there were stages in the geographical movement from Jerusalem to the uttermost parts of the earth, so there were also incremental steps in this ethnic change.

The first involved the spread of the gospel to the Samaritans. When the old Northern Kingdom Israel fell to the Assyrians in 722 BC, multitudes of Jews including the upper classes of Israelite society were exiled. Assyrian captives from other places were brought to Israel to live. Many of the Jews that remained in Palestine intermarried with these Gentiles and were swayed by their pagan religious beliefs. The Samaritans were their offspring. "Half-breeds" both racially and religiously, these people were so detested by later Jews that, by the time of Jesus, a good Jew going from Galilee to Judea crossed the Jordan to travel in Perea rather than to set foot on Samaritan soil. When the believers carried the gospel to the Samaritans, then, they were making a significant move. Although Samaritans had some Jewish blood flowing through their veins, they were one step removed from being true Jews. Likewise, when the believers included them, the church moved one step away from being a narrow, nationalistic sect confined within Judaism.

The second stage of outreach was the spreading of the gospel to the God-fearers. This term was often used to refer to Gentiles who were attracted to first-century Judaism. Impressed with the high ethical standards of the Jews, these had come to accept the monotheistic beliefs of the Jews, and to a limited degree had incorporated some Jewish practices into their own lifestyles. But they had not become full-fledged proselytes, or converts to the Jewish faith. Two impediments stood in the way.

The first barrier to Gentiles becoming a true proselyte was Jewish nationalism. The Jews were recognized not only as a religious group but also as a nation. To become a proselyte, therefore, was a two-sided coin. Positively, conversion was the adopting of the religious faith of the Jews; negatively, it was tantamount to rejecting one's citizenship to become a part of a nation that had been subjugated to Rome. For a Roman army officer such as Cornelius (ch. 10), this was a significant barrier to formal conversion to Judaism.

The second hindrance to Gentiles converting to the Jewish faith was the rite of circumcision, required by the Jews of all proselytes. For many attracted to Judaism, this physical operation was a barrier to full acceptance of the Jewish religion. When the believers carried the gospel to the God-fearers, they were making one more step away from the narrow confines of Judaism. Although God-fearers believed in the God of the Jews, they were, after all, Gentiles. They were one step further removed from Judaism than the Samaritans.

The final stage of the ethnic outreach was the inclusion of Gentiles who had no prior acquaintance or relation with the monotheistic God of Israel. Probably this is the group referred to as the Greeks in Acts 11:19. The breakthrough is complete when these respond to the proclamation about Jesus. By the end of the book of Acts, the overwhelming majority of the converts to Christianity will have come from this group. In the first section of the book of Acts Peter emerges as the dominant character. In this portion others share the limelight with him. Our study will focus on these central personalities.

Stephen

Listed first among the Seven (6:5), Stephen was appointed to resolve the difficulties related to the distribution of food among the needy within the Jerusalem church. Ironically, no details about his service in this role are given. Instead, Luke pictures Stephen as one of the most eloquent preachers of the early church. A man "full of faith and the Holy Spirit" (6:5) and "full of grace and power" (6:8), Stephen forcefully defended his faith against those who rose up to argue with him. Not able to defeat him in debate, they turned to deceit, accusing him of blaspheming both Moses and God. False witnesses against him were enlisted, and he was brought before the Sanhedrin on charges of profaning the temple and the Law. In his defense he delivered the longest speech recorded in the book of Acts (7:2-53).

Scholars have long debated the nature of the speeches in Acts, twenty-four of which occur within the book. Are they verbatim accounts of what was said on the occasion, or are they literary creations of the author? Would impromptu sermons proclaimed on the spur of the moment have been remembered word for word and passed down orally for decades? Or would the gist of what was said be that which was handed down by word of mouth? Since the speeches reflect the same Lukan style and vocabulary that are found in the narrative sections of the book, one should probably conclude that they are primarily Lukan compositions. Though the central theme of a speech may have been preserved in the oral traditions of the church, Luke with his characteristic literary skill fleshed out the idea into the fully formed speech that is recorded in Acts. Ironically, most scholars holding this view make one major exception to this understanding: the speech of Stephen. Because of its length and distinctive ideas, most interpreters conclude that here Luke was using some kind of source.[1]

In his speech Stephen retold the Old Testament story from Abraham to David with a heavy emphasis on Moses. Two main thrusts seem to emerge in this defense.

First, God is not limited to one geographical place. The Israelites were more aware of this fact when they were a pilgrim people, moving the tabernacle, the visible symbol of the presence of God, with them wherever they went. Problems arose when they decided to build the temple, a permanent dwelling for God. In their minds God became tied down to a place—their place in Jerusalem. They felt God was confined to them; they had a monopoly on access to him. The temple was a symbol of Jewish exclusivity. Stephen, then, infuriated the Sanhedrin with the insight that God does not live in temples made by human hands (7:48).

Second, Israel's history reveals a pattern of its rejection of God's leaders. Specifically, Stephen cited as an example the people's rejection of Moses in the wilderness (7:35, 39), even though God had raised him up to be their leader (7:35b-36). Just as their ancestors had rejected the leadership of Moses and the prophets, now the Jews have rejected God's righteous one, Jesus himself (7:52).

In a furious frenzy these Jewish leaders rushed at him, dragged him out of the city, and stoned him to death. Stephen became the first Christian martyr. He died like Jesus: both were tried before the Sanhedrin (Luke 22:66; Acts 6:12); both made statements about the Son of Man positioned at the right hand of God (Luke 22:69; Acts 7:56); both prayed for the forgiveness of those putting them to death (Luke 23:34; Acts 7:60); both commended their spirits to the Divine (Luke 23:46; Acts 7:59); and both were buried by devout men (Luke

23:50-53; Acts 8:2). Once again Luke demonstrates the continuity of the story in Acts with that in the Gospel.

The witness of Stephen marked the first departure from narrow Jewish exclusivity within Christianity. He was the first in the church to realize, or at least to verbalize, the universal implications of the gospel: just as God cannot be confined to one place, God cannot be limited to one people. With the Hellenists, then, and not with the Hebrews, the transition to Gentile Christianity began.

There is one other element in the story we should not overlook. At the execution of this one who first voiced this vision of a worldwide gospel, Luke introduces us to Saul (Paul), the individual who more than any other single person made that vision a reality (7:58).

Philip

Following the death of Stephen, intense persecution erupted against the church (8:2). To escape the violence, they "all" fled from the city of Jerusalem "except for the apostles." Surprising here is the exception. If the church was being persecuted, the last people we would expect to be unaffected were the leaders, the apostles. Yet, they appear to remain unharmed in Jerusalem throughout the remainder of the story recorded in Acts. Reading between the lines, I think we can legitimately conclude that the persecution was directed not towards the church as a whole but to one faction within it: the Hellenists. Controversy had first emerged in a Hellenist synagogue (6:9), and now persecution by fellow Jews was being implemented against them. At the heart of the matter was their understanding of the inclusive nature of God as envisioned by Stephen. The statement "except the apostles" implies that the Twelve did not share this vision. They were still comfortable in the temple and content to proclaim the gospel among the Jews of Jerusalem. Only after inner struggle would some of them hesitatingly come to embrace the worldwide vision of the gospel. The breakthroughs in the spread of the gospel would not come from the Hebrew wing of the church; that story would belong to the Hellenists.

Among these was Philip, who, because of the persecution, fled to Samaria. As we noted earlier, typical Jews avoided even walking through Samaria. Philip was not typical. Not only did he walk though this territory, he audaciously proclaimed the Messiah to the people there. Large numbers of both men and women responded to the message, and they were baptized (8:12). For the first time non-Jews were approached, and they responded positively to the gospel.

When news of these activities reached Jerusalem, the apostles sent Peter and John to Samaria. Why they were sent is not explicitly stated. Did they go to check out the validity of the Samaritan mission? Or was their purpose to affirm it? Whatever the intention, the result was affirmation. The apostles laid their hands on the recently baptized converts, and they received the Holy Spirit (8:17).

At this point we should observe that the accounts of the coming of the Spirit in Acts are not uniformly consistent. At times the receipt of the Spirit is associated with baptism as a part of the conversion experience (2:38). In the Cornelius episode the coming of the Spirit precedes baptism (10:44-48). Here the Spirit comes some time after baptism. At times, as here, the arrival of the Spirit is associated with the laying on of hands. At others, such as at Pentecost, the rite of hand imposition is not mentioned. Consequently, modern Christians should be cautious about imposing any type of sequential order upon the idea of the coming of the Spirit in relationship to baptism, laying on of hands, or any other similar experience. As John Polhill has observed: "The Spirit cannot be tied down to any manipulative human schema."[2]

It is my conviction that one comes to know and confess Christ because of the striving of the Spirit within that one. Indeed one cannot belong to Christ without having the Spirit of God (Rom 8:9). Thus I conclude that the receiving of the Spirit by these Samaritan converts referred to an outward manifestation of the Spirit similar to that experienced by the Jewish believers at Pentecost. In fact, I suspect that the manifestation here was not as much for the benefit of the Samaritans as it was for Peter and John! For these apostles the coming of the Spirit upon the Samaritans was confirmation that these new believers were as fully accepted by God as those in Jerusalem.[3]

Although the Samaritan mission had not originated with them, Peter and John did preach in other Samaritan villages as they returned to Jerusalem. Although they did not take the initiative in going to the Samaritans, they witnessed the divine affirmation of that mission. As a result, they participated in the endeavor themselves. This incident is the last in Acts in which John is a participant. What a fitting conclusion to a less flattering picture of him in Luke's Gospel. When Jesus had begun his journey from Galilee to Jerusalem, he and the disciples were rejected by a Samaritan village. James and John had wanted to call down fire from heaven to destroy the people (Luke 9:51-56). Yet, when Jesus had earlier been rejected at Nazareth (4:16-30), James and John had not suggested destruction of the people. The difference in the two incidents was a matter of race. The Nazarenes were Jews, while the others were Samaritans. James and John had wanted to destroy these people, not simply because of the rejection but because they were Samaritans who had turned Jesus away. Now in Acts, John, reached out and physically touched those whom he previously had wanted to destroy (8:17); and taking his cue from Philip, he gladly preached to them (8:25). Miracles in the New Testament include changed attitudes; contact with Christ can even erase racial prejudice!

After the experience in Samaria, Philip was divinely directed to the road to Gaza where he encountered a eunuch, the treasurer of the queen of Ethiopia (8:26-40). Since the eunuch was avidly reading the scroll of Isaiah on his way home from worshiping in Jerusalem, we can conclude that he was a God-fearer, a Gentile attracted to Judaism without becoming a proselyte. In his particular case he was not allowed to be a full-fledged convert because of his physical condition (Deut 23:1). After Philip's explanation of the Scriptures in the light of their fulfillment in Jesus, the eunuch accepted Christ and asked for baptism. Prevented by the Law from becoming a Jew, he found that there was nothing to hinder him from being a Christian!

The second major stage in the movement from Jewish to Gentile Christianity was pioneered by Philip. Not only did he make the first breakthrough by going to the partially-Jewish Samaritans, he also was the first to proclaim Jesus to a God-fearer!

The final stage in this movement was the outreach to Gentiles who had no prior acquaintance with the God of Israel. Luke describes this development in chapter 11. After a two-chapter interlude in which he discusses the conversions of Saul (ch. 9) and Cornelius (ch. 10), Luke picks up the story of the Hellenists again. Although Philip is not mentioned, people like him, scattered because of the persecution in Jerusalem, brought the gospel to Antioch where they spoke to the "Greeks" about Jesus (11:20).

Antioch in Syria was the third largest city in the Roman Empire, surpassed in size only by Rome and Alexandria. Founded by one of the successors of Alexander the Great, it was from the beginning a thoroughly Greek city. How appropriate, then, is Luke's note that at Antioch the disciples were first called "Christians."

This is not a term the early believers used of themselves; it is found in only two other places in the New Testament (Acts 26:28; 1 Pet 4:16). Instead, it was used by outsiders to describe the followers of Christ. Here in the city where the gospel was first proclaimed to the Gentiles such a term was needed by the Greeks to identify their fellow Gentiles who had become believers. The term "Jews" was no longer appropriate to describe these believers, for indeed these were not Jews or proselytes to Judaism; Christianity was establishing an identity of its own.

Another factor of interest is the composition of the name. "Christian" is formed by adding a Latin ending (*ian*) to the Greek translation (Christ) of a Hebrew concept (Messiah). The name itself has a universal quality. How fitting, then, that this inclusive name was first used in the city where the Gentiles were included among the believers for the first time.

Peter

Philip's ministry to the Samaritans and God-fearers (Acts 8) is followed in the Acts sequence by the account of Saul's conversion (ch. 9). However, I will skip over that narrative to look at the experience of Peter with Cornelius in 10:1–11:18, for Peter's story both complements and stands in contrast to that of Philip.

Cornelius, too, was a God-fearer (10:2). A Roman centurion stationed in Caesarea, he was known as one who was generous to those in need and one who regularly prayed to God. In one of his periods of prayer he had a vision of an angel telling him to search out Simon Peter in the city of Joppa. Immediately he responded, sending representatives to find Peter and to bring him to Caesarea so that Cornelius could hear what he had to say.

At noon the next day Peter also had a vision, but his was somewhat troubling. A sheet was lowered from heaven, suspended by its four corners and holding a menagerie of clean and unclean animals. Hungry Peter heard a voice: "Get up, Peter; kill and eat." Warily, Peter responded that he had never eaten anything unclean; he was not going to fall for a "trick." The heavenly voice reacted: "What God has made clean, you must not call profane." Even more perplexing, the vision was repeated for a total of three times. As Peter was contemplating its meaning, the men arrived with the message from Cornelius.

When Peter heard their request, he went with them as he had been instructed by the Spirit (10:20). When he entered the house of Cornelius, he found the centurion's family and friends waiting. In our last chapter I suggested that when two or three were gathered together, Peter preached. I would have to clarify that now by saying two or three Jews! Peter, at best, was a reluctant witness. To be fair to Peter, I think that some understanding of the meaning of the vision was beginning to sink in, but not the full implications. He began by reminding them that, according to law, he really should not be there. Nevertheless, he had come because God had shown him that he should not call any person unclean. Notice, however, that

Peter did not share the gospel; instead, he asked why Cornelius had sent for him. At Pentecost (ch. 2) and at the temple (ch. 3), he preached to the Jews on the spur of the moment. Here he had a ready-made audience, eager to hear what he had to say, and he asked for explanations.

After Cornelius shared the details of his experience, the light finally dawned for Peter. At last he understood the meaning of the sheet. He was not merely to accept these Gentiles as human beings, but also to accept them as Christian brothers and sisters. He was to preach the gospel to them. As he did, the Holy Spirit came upon them all (10:44), much to the astonishment of those who had come with him from Joppa. Again, I wonder if this manifestation of the Spirit was not actually more for the benefit of Peter and his companions than it was for these God-fearers. Just as he had seen the authentication of the salvation of the Samaritans by the presence of the Spirit, now he saw that these were having the same experience. The gift of the Holy Spirit had been poured out—even upon the Gentiles, just as it had upon Jewish Christians at Pentecost (11:15). Not only had the Hellenists reached out to the God-fearers, but in this event the Hebrews had also.

When Peter returned to Jerusalem and was called on the carpet by the "circumcised believers" for approaching the Gentiles, he told his detractors about the visions and about his subsequent ministry to these God-fearers (11:1-18). He put them to silence when he related the outpouring of the Spirit, concluding that he was not about to hinder the God who gave the same gift of the Spirit to these people that He had given to the Jewish Christians at Pentecost. Even those who had been critical of Peter agreed that "God has given even to the Gentiles the repentance that leads to life" (11:18). Because of subsequent controversies dealing with the acceptance of Gentiles into the church, we probably should not read too much into this exclamation. The Jewish Christians apparently saw the salvation of Cornelius and his friends as a unique experience for which they could praise God, but they did not see it as a pattern that was to be followed in the future. It was an exception rather than a rule.

Luke, however, obviously disagreed. That the story of Cornelius was of crucial importance in his mind is demonstrated by his unusual treatment of it: he records the story, or at least central elements in it, more than one time. This repetition comes as a surprise, for the author was typically highly selective, not telling every incident in the life of the early church, but choosing those that best revealed the understanding of the church he wanted his readers to perceive. Since he did not tell everything, we would not expect him to repeat anything. But he does. His repetitions, furthermore, are even more surprising when we recall the practical problem of scroll length. An author was able to tell only as much as a scroll of manageable length could contain. In this section, however, Luke records three times the vision that came to Cornelius (10:3-6, 30-32; 11:13), and twice he gives the details about the one that came to Peter (10:11-16; 11:5-10).

The initial account of each of these two incidents falls properly within the narrative; Luke is telling the reader what happened. The subsequent accounts are in the form of verbal reports; a speaker is recalling for the benefit of others what has transpired. For the reader, however, these repetitions are unnecessary. For example, in recording the testimony of Peter in 11:5-10 as he spoke to the Jewish Christians back in Jerusalem, Luke could easily have abbreviated the narrative and saved valuable space on the scroll by a statement in the third person: "Peter told them about his vision." The reader, after all, would already know the details. Yet, he repeats the incident in detail. Obviously Luke is stressing for the reader the significance of the event. This turning to the Gentiles is indeed ordained by God.

Paul

Earlier we noted that the two main characters in Acts are Peter and Paul. But they are not given equal treatment in the book. Of the twenty-eight chapters in Acts, Peter is not even mentioned in seventeen of them. After Paul is introduced at the end of chapter 7, on the other hand, only one chapter (10) fails to mention his name. Such an emphasis comes as no surprise. Luke is primarily concerned with the expansion of Christianity to and among the Gentiles. How better to tell the story than to concentrate on the activities of the one person more responsible for this expansion that any other individual?

The last section in our analysis of Acts exclusively features the career of Paul. Yet, he is also prominent in this transitional section. Here the narrative focuses on three different aspects of Paul's life and ministry: conversion, first missionary journey, and the Jerusalem Conference.

Conversion

Earlier we noted Luke's repetition of material to emphasize its importance. Nowhere is this more evident than in his narratives about the conversion of the Apostle to the Gentiles. Three times he tells the story: in a third-person narrative in 9:1-31, and then in first-person accounts on the lips of Paul in 22:1-21 and 26:2-23. For Luke, this experience of Paul was of unparalleled significance in the life of the early church.

Paul is known by two names in this section, first "Saul" and then "Paul." When I was growing up, my Sunday school teachers insisted that Saul's conversion was so dramatic, his name immediately was changed to Paul. Though my teachers had good intentions, I think they were unduly influenced by the accounts of dramatic name changes in the stories of other important biblical figures—Abram to Abraham, Jacob to Israel, and Simon to Peter—and assumed that the phenomenon was repeated in the experience of Paul. The text of Acts, though, gets in the way of this idea, for Luke consistently uses the name Saul in the first part of the story, from the introduction of Saul in chapter 7 to the first missionary journey in chapter 13. In 13:9 Luke mentions that Saul is also known as Paul, and thereafter never uses the former name again. More than likely, the man was given both names at birth: Saul, a Jewish name reflecting his family's religious heritage, and Paul, a Roman name appropriate for his family's social status as Roman citizens. Quite simply, when he was closely associated with the Jewish community in Palestine, he was typically addressed by his Jewish name. In the larger Greco-Roman world, he was usually known as the other. Luke basically reflects this arrangement. The actual shift from Saul to Paul occurs early in the first missionary journey as Paul emerged as the spokesman for the traveling missionaries.

Saul is first introduced at the stoning of Stephen, where, though he was not an active participant, he approved of what was going on (8:1). As the persecution broke out against the Hellenists after Stephen's death, furthermore, Saul played a significant role; in fact, of those wreaking havoc against the church, his is the only name mentioned (8:3). Determined to stamp out the proponents of this inclusive movement, he requested and received letters of recommendation from the high priest to the synagogues in Damascus so he could extend his vendetta there (9:1-3). On his way to this city he had a dramatic confrontation with the risen Jesus.

Nearing Damascus, Saul was knocked to his knees by a blinding light, and he heard the heavenly voice: "Saul, Saul, why do you persecute me?" Unable to see, Saul asked who was speaking. The voice responded, "I am Jesus, whom you are persecuting." Notice that the voice did not ask why Saul was persecuting the church, my followers, or my disciples, but why was he persecuting me? Interesting in this statement is the identification of Jesus with the church. As we later shall see in our study of Paul, one of his favorite metaphors to describe the church is the "body of Christ." Could the roots of that understanding go back to the experience on the Damascus road?

Instructed to proceed into the city, he there awaited a disciple named Ananias who ministered to him, laying his hands on Saul and baptizing him. Saul's sight was restored, and he was filled with the Spirit (9:17-19). Immediately he began to preach in the synagogues that Jesus is the Son of God.

Some have questioned the appropriateness of the term conversion, which means "turning," to describe the experience of Saul. After all, he did not turn from not believing in God to believing; he did not change from being irreligious to being religious; he did not turn from immoral behavior to morality. But he did turn; he did change. Though he did not reject the God of his youth, he came to believe that God had become manifest in Jesus of Nazareth. Convinced of this fact, the persecutor became the proclaimer. The one determined to destroy Christianity became its most eloquent defender.

Paul in his own writings stresses that from the very beginning God had called him to minister to the Gentiles (Gal 1:16). That emphasis is paralleled in the three Lukan accounts of his conversion experience (9:15; 22:21; 26:17). Though minor details vary from one narrative to the other, the basic thrust is the same: Paul's destiny was with the Gentiles. To be sure, Paul was not the first to share the gospel with Gentiles; but both in Acts and in church history he was certainly the most significant person to do so.

In one sense Saul's conversion paralleled that of Cornelius. God went to extraordinary means—such as visions—to facilitate their responses to the message of the gospel. But these are not isolated experiences. In the salvation of every person, whether accompanied by dramatic phenomena or not, God takes the initiative (Eph 1:4-5). Not everyone responds positively to God's invitation; but lack of human response does not negate the fact that God takes the first step towards us, not we towards him.

After his conversion Saul remained in the Damascus area for some time. Galatians 1:18 indicates three years, but Luke is not so explicit (cf. Acts 9:23). Saul then returned to Jerusalem for a get-acquainted visit with the church, although many believers were not very confident in his professed Christian belief. Could the one who formerly had tried to destroy them actually have become one of them? Barnabas came to his aid, however, persuading the community of Saul's sincerity, and they accepted Paul into the community. As he preached in Jerusalem, he, too, incurred the threats of some of the Jews, and he was sent to Tarsus, his hometown, for reasons of safety (9:30).

At this point in the Acts chronology Luke shifts his attention back to Peter (9:32–11:18). Nothing is said about Saul's activities in this period. Later, a quick reference is made to him in chapter 11. After the Hellenists preached directly to the Gentiles in Antioch, the Jerusalem church sent Barnabas to investigate. Overwhelmed by the response to the gospel in this city, Barnabas sent word to Tarsus for Saul to come and to assist him in leading this new Christian community. Here they labored together for a year (11:26).

First Missionary Journey

After taking a famine relief offering to the needy believers in Jerusalem (11:29), Barnabas and Saul returned once again to Antioch (12:25). Here a new challenge awaited them. Inspired by the Holy Spirit, the church set them apart for special service and sent them off on what is generally called "the first missionary journey." Previously, Luke has been preparing the reader for what now was about to take place. He has developed the story of a movement born within Judaism that quickly spread unhindered to Samaritans, God-fearers, and even to some with no prior knowledge of God. Further, he has dramatically related the conversion of the one called to champion the outreach to the Gentiles. Now he indicates that the church in Antioch set Barnabas and Saul apart for the work to which God had "called" them (13:2). The outreach to the Gentiles is divinely ordained! We should not overlook the fact that the church in Antioch, not the one in Jerusalem, took the initiative in sending out this first missionary team. Again, it was the Hellenist wing of the church that was the driving force in carrying out the commission given to the apostles by Jesus (1:8). With their appointment of Barnabas and Saul for this task, the stage was set for the mission to the Gentiles to begin in earnest!

Taking with them John Mark, Barnabas's young cousin, Barnabas and Saul set sail from Seleucia, the port city for Antioch. Since Cyprus lies close to the Syrian coast, and since

Barnabas was a native of Cyprus (4:36), the island was a convenient place to begin. Going from one end of the island to the other, the missionary pair proclaimed the gospel in the Jewish synagogues. Luke indicates nothing of the reception they received or the response to their preaching. At the far end of the island they encountered Bar-Jesus, a Jewish false prophet who opposed the missionary team and whom Paul condemned, and the Roman proconsul Sergius Paulus who believed. This negative response of the Jew and the positive reaction of this Gentile governor is a preview of what is to come. Paul will preach to Jews as well as to Gentiles, but he will experience rejection from the former and find success among the latter.

Two other developments of note take place at the end of Luke's account of the Cyprus mission. In 13:9 Luke shifts from using the Jewish name "Saul" to the Roman name "Paul." Before this verse every reference to this character has identified him as "Saul"; after this verse preference will be given to "Paul."

One other shift, subtle but significant, occurs in this passage. In previous references to this missionary pair Luke has referred to them as Barnabas and Saul; but from this point on he typically will call them Paul and Barnabas. The order of names within pairs is important; the first is seen as more significant than the second. Barnabas, who had befriended Saul in Jerusalem and engaged him as an assistant in Antioch, was the leader of the missionary team in the beginning. But with the Bar-Jesus incident, Paul emerged as permanent spokesman and leader.

From Cyprus, the team sailed to the coast of south central Asia Minor. Without explanation Luke indicates that here Mark left them to return to Jerusalem. Paul and Barnabas proceeded to Antioch (Pisidia) where on the Sabbath Paul preached in the synagogue (13:16-41). Impressing many of the Jews and proselytes, Paul was invited to speak again the next week. When he and Barnabas returned, however, they were confronted by a group of Jews jealous of the pair's popularity. The Jews challenged and contradicted the preaching of

Paul. As a result, he publicly proclaimed his deliberate turning to the Gentiles, quoting a prophecy from Isaiah to support his intentions (13:46-47). With these Gentiles, then, he found immediate success. Finally, by stirring up opposition among the leading citizens, the Jews drove Paul and Barnabas from the city.

At Iconium, their next stop, the pattern repeated itself. Initial success in preaching in the synagogue was followed by hostile reaction from the unbelieving Jews who stirred up the residents against the missionary team. Learning of a plot to stone them, they escaped from this city and went to Lystra.

Paralleling the experience of Peter in raising the lame man in the temple (ch. 3), Paul at Lystra did the same thing for another man crippled from birth (14:10). Popular reaction among the pagans included the mistaken assumption that Zeus and Hermes, leading Greek gods, had come to Lystra in human form. Initially, the crowds wished to worship Paul and Barnabas. Shortly, the Jews from Antioch and Iconium arrived to stir up opposition, but they incited the crowds to stone Paul instead! Though seriously injured and left for dead, Paul recovered and went to Derbe with Barnabas to preach.

After a successful preaching mission in that city, Paul and Barnabas retraced their steps to Lystra, Iconium, and Antioch. From Derbe, Paul could have taken a more direct route to the east to return to Syrian Antioch. Instead, at great risk to himself, he elected to go back to these cities where he had established Christian communities, but where he had also faced sizable opposition. Evidently he was more concerned with strengthening and encouraging these fledgling communities than he was with his own personal safety. By his own example he demonstrated what he proclaimed: "It is through many persecutions that we must enter the kingdom of God" (14:22).

When the missionary team reached the coast, surprisingly they sailed directly to Antioch and not to Cyprus. If Paul was concerned enough with strengthening converts that he returned to these cities in Asia Minor, why did he not return to the island where the missionary venture had begun? We must remember that travel conditions then were not the same as those today. No passenger ships sailed the Mediterranean; would-be passengers booked passage on merchant ships that just happened to be in port. Perhaps when Paul and Barnabas arrived at the dock, no ships were sailing to Cyprus, but one was available for a voyage to Antioch. Since that was their ultimate destination, and since they had no guarantee about how long they might have to wait for a ship to Cyprus, they secured passage on the vessel sailing to Antioch.

Arriving in the city from which they had first departed, Paul and Barnabas reported on their journey, rejoicing in all that God had accomplished with them. The key phrase in their testimony was that on this preaching mission God had opened a door of faith for the Gentiles (14:27). In Cyprus and Asia Minor, the initial approach taken by the pair had been to preach in the synagogues. Here they hoped to find an audience prepared for their message because these Jews already believed in God and accepted the Scriptures that the Christians believed had been fulfilled in Jesus Christ. Response to their proclamation, though, came primarily from the Gentiles, not from the Jews. The latter, in fact, had provoked considerable opposition to their proclamation. But the door slammed by the Jews was now opened for the Gentiles. The setting for the triumph of Christianity among the Gentiles had been established.

Jerusalem Conference

One major impediment stood in the way of the establishment of Christianity among the Gentiles, however: not the opposition of the Jews, but the limited vision of Jewish Christians. When all Christians were Jews, there was no major problem of identity. These people saw themselves as good Jews who had come to recognize the Way.[4] For them, God had revealed the divine in Jesus, who was indeed the promised Messiah. These believers still worshiped in the temple and the synagogues; they still observed the regulations of the Law. They were practicing Jews who had come to accept Christ as the fulfillment of their age-old expectations and hopes. For these, acceptance of the gospel by the Samaritans and by Cornelius were isolated incidents that were exceptions to the norm expected in the Jewish Christian community.

For these Christian Jews who tended to evaluate everyone's experience in the light of their own, Paul's preaching mission created a crisis. Although he and Barnabas had proclaimed Christ to Jews, they were more successful in winning Gentiles. For Paul, acceptance of the Gentiles had become the norm, not an exception. The objection of the Jewish Christians actually was not to Paul's acceptance of Gentiles per se, but to his unqualified acceptance of these converts. He had not required them to become Jews as a prerequisite for their becoming Christians. From their perspective, Christianity was a movement within Judaism; thus the Jewish Christians saw that it was both logical and necessary that Gentiles first become Jews in order to become Christians. Specifically, they epitomized the issue with the one word circumcision. That ancient ritual dating back to Abraham was a requirement for all proselytes. Therefore, they decreed that a person must be circumcised in order to be saved: one must become a Jew in order to be a Christian (15:1, 5).

When this group advocating circumcision brought this message to Antioch to challenge the authenticity of the Christianity practiced there, dissension and debate ensued. Finally Paul and Barnabas and some unnamed others were appointed to go to Jerusalem to discuss the matter with the apostles. This conference in Jerusalem (c. AD 49) is arguably the most significant meeting in the history of the church, for it established the principle by which Christianity "moved beyond Judaism and became a separate religion reaching the ends of the earth," according to Raymond Brown.[5]

The New Testament contains two accounts of this meeting: this one in Acts 15:4-29 and Paul's version in Galatians 2:1-10. Minor details vary in the two accounts because one was written by a participant just a few years after the event, while the other was written thirty to thirty-five years later by one who was not present and therefore dependent on reports of others. Nevertheless, the two accounts agree on the central issues . The same major personalities (Paul and Barnabas representing Antioch; Peter and James representing Jerusalem) met in Jerusalem to discuss the same issue (circumcision), and they arrived at the same conclusion (circumcision was unnecessary for the Gentile converts).

After the issue was raised by the advocates of circumcision (15:5), Peter reflected on his experience with Gentiles. Without calling the centurion by name, Peter reminded the group of his earlier report about Cornelius. The salvation of that man, his friends, and his family—without circumcision—was authenticated by the Holy Spirit. Although he did not mention his vision of the sheet full of animals at the conference, that experience must have been very much on his mind, for he mentioned that God cleansed the hearts of these God-fearers by faith (15:9). The word "cleansed" is the same term used by the heavenly voice in the vision : "Don't call anything unclean (common) that God has cleansed [made clean]" (10:15, author's paraphrase).

Next to speak were Paul and Barnabas who shared their experiences among the Gentiles. Finally and surprisingly, the last and seemingly authoritative opinion was expressed by James, heretofore mentioned only one time in Acts. This brother of Jesus (Gal 1:19) concluded that what had occurred among the Gentiles was in accordance with the Scriptures (Amos 9:11-12); consequently, they should be accepted without the requirement of circumcision.

Interesting here is the inclusion of James in the narrative. Since he among all the participants spoke last, it is generally concluded that he was the person with the greatest authority, even exceeding that of Peter! Explicitly in his speech he used such words as "I have reached the decision" (Acts 15:19), and his decision was evidently affirmed by the whole church. A hint of this transition from Peter to James in the role of leadership may be seen in 12:17, where Peter mentioned only him by name in a message he sent "to James and to the believers." After this incident Peter is not mentioned again in Acts; and when Paul later returned to Jerusalem (ch. 21), James was the obvious leader of the community there.

James further suggested that some social regulations should be imposed on the Gentiles. Although they did not have to become Jews, it was appropriate that they should observe some minimal requirements: to abstain from blood, the meat of strangled animals, the meat of animals sacrificed to idols, and incestuous relationships (probably the meaning here of the term often translated as "fornication"). These requirements were based on instructions found in Leviticus 17–18 for aliens who lived in Israel. Gentile converts, like aliens in Old Testament times, were not subject to all the Jewish laws and practices; but these were the very minimum customs that these folk should observe so they would not be offensive to the Jewish majority. These regulations had nothing to do with salvation, but they did establish social procedures that should be followed by the Gentiles as they mingled with the Jews in the church.

On of the more serious problems of identifying the conference of Acts 15 with the conference of Galatians 2 is the omission of these regulations from the account Paul gives. Even the Acts presentation is somewhat problematic. When Paul returned to Jerusalem, James informed him of the imposition of these regulations on the Gentiles as if Paul were unaware. Perhaps Luke had conflated two events—the conference and the giving of these rules. If this was the case, Paul and Barnabas left the conference with the decision that circumcision was not necessary for the Gentile converts. Later, in the communities under the influence of James, that is, churches that were predominantly Jewish Christian, these regulations were proscribed to regulate social relations between the Jewish majority and Gentile minority within the church. For the churches under Paul's influence, those predominantly Gentile congregations, the rules were not observed, for they were unnecessary. If this was the case, the information James gave to Paul in Acts 21 was relevant; James was informing him of current social practice in Jewish Christian circles where Gentile converts had become a part of the community.[6]

This section ends as Paul and Barnabas with representatives of the Jerusalem church returned to Antioch to report the conclusions reached at the conference. The news, not surprisingly, was received with rejoicing. The Christians in Antioch, Jews and Greeks alike, were recognized on equal footing by the mother church in Jerusalem. Furthermore, the mission that the Antioch community had undertaken with the sending of Paul and Barnabas had been vindicated. In Christ there is neither Jew nor Gentile (Gal 3:28).

Conclusion

In many respects this transitional section, 6:8–15:35, is the key portion of the book of Acts. Here Luke records the major innovations that transform Christianity from a Palestinian Jewish sect into an inclusive worldwide movement. As he describes the activities of various personalities, he skillfully alternates episodes involving Peter, the primary character in the first section of the book, with those that feature other influential Christians. In fact, while reading this section we become so acclimated by the diminishing emphasis on Peter that we hardly miss him in the last half of the book. At the same time the author shifts the attention away from Peter, he introduces Paul and begins gradually to trace the development of his increasingly significant role in the expansion of the first-century church. With the ascendancy of the role of Paul, the establishment of a precedent for outreach in the first missionary journey, and the decision of the Jerusalem Conference confirming the inclusion of the Gentiles, we are prepared for the triumph of Gentile Christianity that follows.

Notes

[1]For an excellent recent survey of the issues related to the speeches, see John B. Polhill, *Acts*, The New American Commentary, vol. 26 (Nashville: Broadman, 1992) 43-47.

[2]Ibid., 218.

[3]Interesting here is the fact that the same kind of manifestation of the Spirit is found in the Cornelius episode (10:44-48), where

again Peter witnesses divine authentication of the acceptance of God-fearers.

[4]In Acts "the Way" is a frequent designation for Christianity.

[5]Raymond E. Brown, *An Introduction to the New Testament*, The Anchor Bible Reference Library (New York: Doubleday, 1997) 306.

[6]Ibid., 308-309.

Triumph of Gentile Christianity
(15:36–28:31)

At the end of the narrative about the Jerusalem Conference, Paul emerges as the central character for the last
half of Acts. That Luke's concerns are not primarily biographical becomes obvious in this section, for he does not
mention Peter again after the Conference, and he leaves the
story of Paul open-ended at the conclusion of the book.
Luke's purpose is to help the church to clarify its self-understanding, to explain how it came to be the predominantly
Gentile movement it was at the end of the first century. Run-
ning through his narrative is the idea that nothing could stop
the spread of the gospel. Luke's story is that the gospel
triumphed in spite of religious, nationalistic, racial, geographical, cultural, and political barriers.[1] Certainly, this
unhindered spread of Christianity is nowhere better exempli-
fied than in the career of Paul. Thus Luke concentrates on
Paul's ministry for the remainder of his book.

Typically, Paul's career in Acts is divided into three missionary journeys and then a journey as a prisoner to Rome.
In fact, Bibles often include maps that trace for the reader the
four itineraries. Since the term "journey" connotes the idea
of traveling from one place to another, it accurately describes
the first and the last of these four trips. In the mission to
Cyprus and central Asia Minor (chaps. 13–14) and in the
voyage to Rome (chaps. 27–28), Paul did move progressively
from place to place, never staying long in one location. The

"second and third missionary journeys" do not fit the pattern. During these "journeys" Paul settled down for extended periods in Corinth (for eighteen months) and in Ephesus (for almost three years). He was no longer constantly on the move. Since both of these cities border the Aegean Sea, perhaps the Aegean mission is a better term than missionary journeys for Paul's activity after the Jerusalem Conference.

In addition to the Aegean mission (15:41–21:16), this last section of the book examines the arrest of Paul in Jerusalem with his subsequent imprisonment in Caesarea (21:17–26:32) and finally his voyage as a prisoner to Rome (27:1–28:31).

Aegean Mission

Sometime after their return to Antioch from the Jerusalem Conference, Paul proposed and Barnabas agreed that they should return to check on the churches they had established on their previous journey. Barnabas in turn suggested that John Mark assist them once again. When Paul adamantly insisted that he would not take John Mark along, he and Barnabas parted company. Actually, Luke here has probably simplified the disagreement between Paul and Barnabas, making John Mark the only issue of contention. In Galatians 2:11-14, however, Paul indicates that in Antioch after the Conference, he had publicly confronted Peter for his two-faced treatment of the Gentiles regarding Jewish food laws. Apparently, Peter had originally agreed with Paul that these dietary requirements were not binding on the Gentiles; but when representatives from among the Jewish Christians in Jerusalem arrived on the scene, Peter quickly adopted their stance, which was just the opposite of what he had been practicing. Much to Paul's disappointment, even Barnabas sided with the stricter requirements for the Gentiles. Could it be that this was the more pressing issue that drove a wedge between the two missionary partners? It is probable that Paul was uncomfortable with a more conservative approach to the Gentiles that both Barnabas and Mark advocated.

At any rate, the former companions separated and evidently divided the mission between themselves: Barnabas sailed to Cyprus, and Paul went overland through Syria and Silicia to the churches of south central Asia Minor. All of the territory covered on the first journey was visited by one of the two former partners. Each of them quite naturally visited the place of his birth. Barnabas, the "Son of Consolation" who habitually spoke up for the underdog, took John Mark with him. On the other hand, Paul chose a new traveling partner, Silas, who had earlier accompanied Paul and Barnabas as they returned to Antioch from the Jerusalem Conference (15:32). After the departure of Barnabas and Mark, incidentally, neither is mentioned again in Acts. The story instead centers on the activities of Paul and Silas.

As these two visited Lystra, they met Timothy, a young believer of mixed parentage; his mother was a Jewish Christian, and his father a Greek. Timothy joined the missionary team. By a circuitous route the trio arrived at Troas on the northwest coast of Asia Minor. Twice Luke indicates that the group's intended itinerary was altered by the Holy Spirit (16:6) or the Spirit of Jesus (16:7). Specifically how the Spirit prevented them from traveling to particular areas is not clear. Obviously for Luke, God was directing their movements. They were kept from a ministry in the Roman province of Asia because God wanted them to go to Greece (16:10).

At Troas, Paul had the vision of the Macedonian imploring him to come to that region to help them. Convinced that this was God's call, Paul and his companions set sail for Macedonia. Much has been said about this significant crossing of the Aegean Sea, for hereby Paul left the continent of Asia and carried his message to Europe. Paul's alighting in Macedonia, however, did not mark the arrival of Christianity in Europe. When Paul won converts in Philippi, we can say that these were his first converts in Europe, but not the first converts in Europe. As a matter of fact, we do not know how and when Christianity came to Europe; but based on Paul's comments in his letter to the Roman church, he seems to be writing to a stable church that has been in existence for quite some time, not one founded after his arrival in Macedonia.[2] Also of interest in the narrative here is the presence of the first "we" passage (16:10-17). Again, traditional interpretation has identified the author of Acts as one present with Paul at the time he traveled from Troas to Philippi. Perplexing, though, is the fact that the "we" (and thus the presumed eyewitness) disappears right in the middle of the narrative about one of the incidents in this city.

Converts in Philippi included Lydia, a God-fearer who was a prominent businesswoman in the city (16:13-15), and the unnamed Philippian jailer (16:25-34). Especially significant was Lydia. Not only was she the first of Paul's converts in Europe, but also she was the first of several leading women in this section of Acts who made a positive response to Paul's message of salvation.[3] In Paul's letters we often see women mentioned in roles of leadership; so in Acts women were among Paul's earliest and most significant converts and fellow workers.

Here in Philippi, Paul underwent his first incarceration. Arrested and beaten in response to some questionable charges, Paul was thrown into prison where he experienced a miraculous deliverance (16:25-26) that paralleled the similar experiences of Peter (5:19; 12:6-11). Furthermore, in Luke's account of the incident we have the first indication that Paul was a Roman citizen (16:37). When he complained to the magistrates about the unjust treatment that he, a citizen, had received, they apologized and asked him to leave the city.

Hostility again confronted Paul as he moved on to Thessalonica (17:1-9) and Berea (17:10-14), but in these places the conflict was instigated by Thessalonian Jews jealous of Paul's successful preaching. Leaving Timothy and Silas in Macedonia, Paul traveled alone to Athens, the intellectual center of the ancient world. Here Paul shared the gospel with people in the marketplace, including Epicurean and Stoic philosophers. When he mentioned resurrection, these in particular were offended, for with very minimalist ideas about life after death, they could not conceive of a resurrection of the body.[4] For a more formal opportunity to share his views, they took him to the Areopagus (Mars Hill), either a hill below the famous Acropolis or an Athenian court whose name was derived from this site. Here he delivered his most famous speech found in the book of Acts (17:22-31). Taking as his starting point the monument the Athenians had erected to the "unknown god," Paul approached the topic of his monotheistic creator God using philosophical and poetic allusions with which they were familiar. The audience evidently listened patiently until Paul again referred to the idea of resurrection (17:31), a concept that caused many to scoff. His sermon, though, bore some fruit in that some of the leading citizens became believers (17:34).

Paul's next stop was Corinth, the largest city in Greece. Visits to the other major Greek cities—Philippi, Thessalonica, and Athens—had been brief, but here Paul spent the next eighteen months. Several features of Luke's brief account of this lengthy period stand out. First, in Corinth, Paul met and then lived and worked with Aquila and Priscilla, Jewish Christians from Rome who became his lifetime colleagues.

Second, Paul repeated the pattern from his earlier visits to other cities of going first to the synagogue to proclaim the gospel. Just as in his experiences in Thessalonica and Berea, Paul again encountered a hostile reaction from the Jews. What Luke has implied in his narrative of other incidents of Jewish rejection he now states explicitly: in the face of this Jewish opposition, Paul pointedly and intentionally turned to the Gentiles (18:5-6). Striving to clarify the church's self-understanding at the end of the first century, Luke has reiterated that Christianity became predominantly Gentile not because the church had neglected the Jews in its missionary outreach, but because Jews usually had rejected the gospel.

Finally, the episode at Corinth is of particular significance for establishing a chronology of Paul's life. Jews in the city brought charges against Paul before the Roman proconsul (governor) Gallio who dismissed the case because it dealt with internal religious squabbles of Jews instead of matters concerning the state. Not one of the main characters in the story, Gallio has become significant in twentieth-century biblical study because of an inscription addressed to him found near Delphi, Greece, near the beginning of this century. Although the inscription does not contain a date, it does have dateable information that has established Gallio as proconsul of Achaia in AD 51–52. Since Paul appeared before Gallio, this year has become pivotal for establishing the dates for Paul's life.[5]

In Luke's accounts of Paul's ministry in Philippi, Thessalonica, and Berea he states the circumstances that caused Paul to leave those places. At the end of the Corinthian mission, though, like that in Athens, the author simply states that Paul went elsewhere. We should remember that Luke has been selective in the materials he has recorded; he has not tried to give the reader every detail. Some of these, however, are supplied by Paul's own writings. As he describes his travel plans in his letter to the church at Rome, for example, Paul indicates that at times he feels his work in a particular area is complete and it is time to move on (Rom 15:23). Evidently, Paul thought his work in Corinth was finished. Earlier Luke indicated that Paul had wanted to go into Asia but had been prevented by the Holy Spirit (16:6). Consequently, we are not surprised to see here that when Paul decided to leave Corinth, he went to Ephesus, the leading city in Asia.

Actually, he left Priscilla and Aquila in Ephesus, perhaps to initiate the work there, as he traveled on to Palestine for brief visits to Jerusalem and to Antioch (18:18-22). When he began his return trip to Ephesus, he traveled overland so he could revisit the churches of Galatia on his way.

While Paul was traveling to Ephesus, Apollos, an eloquent Alexandrian Jewish Christian, arrived in the city. Apollos had been instructed in the way of the Lord and had accurately and enthusiastically taught about Jesus, he evidently was not aware of Christian baptism (18:24-25). Further instruction he received from Priscilla and Aquila (18:16).

We should notice the order of the names of the husband and wife here: Priscilla is listed first! Typically when a husband and wife are listed in the first-century documents, the husband's name is mentioned before the wife's, reflecting their roles in the social order of that day. The reverse sequence here would have been immediately obvious to the original readers. We should also remember that rank or importance is indicated when any two names are linked together. In Acts 13, for example, the subtle but notable shift in name order from "Barnabas and Saul" to "Paul and Barnabas" indicates that Paul had superseded Barnabas in significance. In Acts 18:2 Aquila and Priscilla are introduced in traditional order, but in 18:18 and 18:26 the order is reversed. Similarly, though Paul mentions the couple in traditional fashion in 1 Corinthians 16:19 (he normally calls Priscilla "Prisca"), elsewhere in his letters he also reverses the sequence (Rom 16:3; 2 Tim 4:19). Although Paul calls both of them his co-workers (Rom 16:3), he evidently recognizes, as does Luke, that the wife was the more significant of the two. In Acts 18:26 Priscilla and her husband instructed a man who was already well informed about the faith!

After Paul arrived in Ephesus, he spent three years in this city—his longest stay in any one place mentioned in the book of Acts. Ironically, very little, proportionately, is recorded about his experiences in this significant cultural center. Again Paul began his work in the synagogue, proclaiming boldly for three months his understanding of the kingdom of God. Finally, after a disruption caused by nonbelieving Jews, he withdrew to a lecture hall where for two years he expounded the gospel for both Jews and Greeks (19:8-10).

Paul's Ephesian mission flourished, as Luke illustrates with two incidents. First, Paul's ministry had an impact on those practicing magic and divination. Rejecting these rituals as they accepted Christ, these practitioners burned their magic books, which, Luke adds, were worth fifty thousand silver coins (19:19). Second, Paul's success in winning converts raised the ire of the local silversmiths. Their lucrative sale of silver shrines of Artemis, the patron goddess, was being threatened by the popularity of this message that gods made by human hands were not really deities. In fact, these artisans even feared for the stability of the local cultic worship of Artemis in the magnificent temple erected to her just outside their city. A near riot erupted as these tradesmen incited the crowds gathered in the theater to protest this threat to their culture and their economy. This raucous assembly was finally quieted and dismissed by the town clerk who suggested that such disputes should be settled by the courts, not a riotous mob (19:23-41).

Before the riot Paul had already planned on leaving the city (19:21-22). After the episode in the theater he departed for Macedonia (Philippi, Thessalonica, and Berea) and Achaia (Athens and Corinth) with the intention of sailing on to Antioch in Syria (20:1-3). At this point Paul was evidently collecting the money he ultimately wanted to take to the poor among the saints in Jerusalem (Rom 15:25-26), but Luke is silent about this collection, either because he is unaware of this offering or because the collection strategy was unsuccessful. Luke does, however, record the itinerary Paul followed as he undertook this endeavor.[6]

When Paul learned of a Jewish plot against him, he changed his intended itinerary, retracing his steps to Macedonia from which he sailed to Asia Minor. After a week in Troas, he traveled down the coast, deliberately bypassing Ephesus, perhaps because he knew it would be difficult to leave the church there again. Since his return to Greece lasted more than three months, he probably feared further delays if he made a farewell visit to Ephesus. Consequently, he requested the elders of the Ephesian church to meet him in Miletus (20:7-18).

In this setting Paul delivered his third major speech or sermon within the context of his missionary activities in Acts (20:18-35). The first was to Jews in the synagogue in Pisidian Antioch (13:16-41); the second was the Areopagus address to Gentiles in Athens (17:22-31). This final one he delivered to believers, Ephesian church leaders who had assembled in Miletus to bid him farewell. Unlike the evangelistic outreach of his earlier speeches and the legal defenses he gives later (22:1-21; 26:2-23), this address as recorded in Acts has much in common with the thought and language of his epistles that also, as a matter of fact, are addressed to believers. After reviewing his ministry with them (20:18-21) and acknowledging the dangers that yet lay before him (20:22-27), Paul admonished the elders to be cautious and selfless shepherds of the flock entrusted to them (20:28-35).

Luke concludes this section with brief notes on Paul's itinerary from Miletus to Jerusalem (21:1-16). The great Aegean mission was finished. Paul approached a new phase of his ministry, hoping to go to Rome after a visit in Jerusalem (19:21), but keenly aware of dangers that might await him in Jerusalem (20:22; 21:4, 10-13).

With the close of the Aegean mission, Luke's presentation of the church's mission to the Gentiles has reached its climax. Although reminders of this mission are found in the remaining narratives, most of the text is not concerned so much with outreach to Gentiles as it is with the scenes of Paul's arrest, incarceration, defense, and journey to Rome as a prisoner.[7]

Arrest and Imprisonment

Paul's arrival in Jerusalem was met with mixed response from the Christian community. On the one hand Paul and his companions were received warmly by the "brothers" (21:17), yet on the other hand James and the other elders were more cautious. They rejoiced with Paul as he reported what had transpired in his Aegean mission, a ministry to the Gentiles that the Jerusalem church basically had affirmed in the Jerusalem Conference. But their response to Paul was also colored by a degree of hesitancy. Paul's success among the Gentiles was somewhat of a liability for them in their outreach to the Jews.

Chronologically, Paul's arrival in Jerusalem probably occurred about AD 56–57, during the period that Felix ruled in Palestine as procurator. This was a time of fervent Jewish nationalism fostering hostile feelings towards Gentiles in general and the Roman overlords in particular. Word of Paul's vigorous outreach to Gentiles would not set well with the unbelieving Jews to whom the Jerusalem church was trying to minister. Why would these Jews want to be part of a movement catering to these despicable outsiders?[8] To make matters worse for their perception of Paul, it had actually been reported that he had encouraged Jews living among the Gentiles to forsake circumcision and the other customs deemed essential for Jewish identity by the Jerusalem populace (21:21).

Seeking to mollify the Jerusalem Jews, the elders suggested that Paul participate in a Nazarite ceremony in the temple in order to disprove the rumors that he encouraged Jews to violate the law of Moses. Paul agreed. When he entered the temple, though, hostile Jews who had seen him earlier with one of his Gentile converts, accused him of violating the temple by bringing Gentiles into the restricted temple courts. A riot broke out (21:22-30).

Rescued from the mob by a Roman tribune, Paul was arrested, but was allowed to address the people. When they heard him speaking in Aramaic, their native tongue, the crowd grew quiet and listened. Basically, Paul stressed his Jewish credentials and described his earlier zealous attempts to persecute the followers of the Way (22:3-5). In a vivid first person account he then related the events of his conversion, a story already known to the reader from Luke's earlier, more detailed version recorded in chapter 9. All remained quiet with the crowd until Paul indicated that Jesus had commissioned him to go to the Gentiles. Hearing that word, they exploded in fury once again, and Paul was taken away to the military barracks by the Romans.

Since he did not quite understand the reaction of the Jews to Paul, the tribune summoned the Sanhedrin for a hearing so they could develop formal charges against the prisoner. This meeting, too, gave way to violent dissension when Paul deliberately mentioned the issue of resurrection, a notion about which there was no agreement among the Sadducees and the Pharisees on the council (23:1-10). After he returned to the barracks, Paul learned of a plot by forty Jews to kill him when he was taken again before the council. Upon hearing of the planned ambush, the tribune whisked Paul away to Caesarea, the Roman seat of government, so that the procurator Felix could handle the situation (23:11-35).

A formal delegation of Jews from Jerusalem brought charges against Paul, but Felix postponed a decision. Luke indicates that Felix was well informed about the Christian movement and implied that he found no basis for the charges against Paul. Rather, Felix delayed judgment, hoping Paul would offer him a bribe (24:26). Under these conditions Paul remained in prison for two years.

In AD 60, Porcius Festus succeeded Felix as governor. Learning about Paul's case, Festus arranged another hearing in Caesarea and, to placate the Jews, suggested a formal trial in Jerusalem. Paul, though, fearing Jewish plots—they still had plans for an ambush (25:3)—appealed his case to the emperor. Shortly thereafter, Herod Agrippa II, great-grandson of Herod the Great, visited Festus. Since Agrippa would have a better understanding of the religious situation than Festus, the governor asked his guest to interview Paul so he could prepare formal written charges to accompany his prisoner to Rome.

In presenting his case before Festus and Agrippa, Paul described his background as a devout Jew who formerly persecuted the church but who was confronted by the risen Jesus on the road to Damascus. Thus for the third time Paul's conversion experience is recorded in Luke's narrative (26:2-23). After hearing the prisoner, Agrippa concluded there was no basis to the charges against Paul and that he could have been set free if he had not appealed his case to the emperor (26:31-32). Two features of this presentation should be noted. First, Luke has again intimated a parallel between the experience of Jesus and that of his followers. In the Gospel, Jesus was tried before a Roman governor, Pilate, who arranged a hearing for the prisoner before a Herod (Luke 23:6-12). Likewise, Paul faced the Roman governor Festus who arranged a hearing before another Herod. Even towards the end of his narrative, Luke stresses the continuity of the story in Acts with the story he recorded in his first book. Second, we should not overlook Paul's reiteration of the fact that he was called to proclaim the good news to the Gentiles (26:20). In fact, he indicated, this ministry to the Gentiles was the reason

for the Jewish hostility against him (v. 21). Generally, in this
last section of Luke's narrative Paul was a prisoner no longer
able to engage in extensive missionary activity. Yet, Luke does
not let the reader forget that the church's inclusion of the
Gentiles is central to the story he has sought to tell, but also
that it is grounded in the intention and initiative of God.

Voyage to Rome

The final two chapters in Acts describe Paul's voyage as a
prisoner to Rome. To the emperor he had appealed; to the
emperor, then, he had to go (25:12). For the final time the
narrative is recorded in the first person plural. The journey is
recorded in great detail, with vivid comments about naviga-
tion and very specific geographical references. Booking
passage on merchant ships, the party of Roman centurion,
prisoners, and companions sailed up the Syrian coast, turned
west along the southern coast of Asia Minor, and docked
briefly at Fair Havens on Crete. Hoping to find a better port
in which to spend the winter, they again set sail, thereby
encountering a ferocious storm at sea that finally left them
shipwrecked on the island of Malta. While wintering there,
Paul again reached out to the Gentiles, healing the father of
the leading citizen and ministering to the natives (28:1-9).

Sailing on another ship in the spring, the party finally
docked in Italy, with Paul receiving a warm welcome from
the believers. Among the Christians, evidently, his reputation
and the expectation of his arrival had preceded him (28:14-
15). Jews in the area, however, seem to have heard little about
him (28:21), but were interested in hearing his message.
Living under the conditions of house arrest (28:16), Paul was
able to receive visitors in great numbers, and on an appointed
day Jews came to hear what he had to say. Similar to his experiences elsewhere, particularly Pisidian Antioch, some of the
Jews believed while others remained unconvinced. Though
Luke does not explicitly say so, Paul's words to the Jews as
they departed indicate that the unbelievers outnumbered the
believers. Paul found their reaction resonant with the words
of the call vision of Isaiah (Isa 6:9-10). He responded that

though these unbelieving Jews had rejected the salvation he had proclaimed, the Gentiles would listen!

At the beginning (Pisidian Antioch), at the middle (Corinth), and at the end (Rome) of Luke's account of Paul's missionary career, he notes that Jewish rejection of Paul's message resulted in a deliberate turning to the Gentiles (13:46; 18:6; 28:28). Let us not forget that Luke was writing to aid the self-understanding of the late first-century church. Why was it predominantly Gentile, although its roots went back to truest Judaism? Luke demonstrated from the life of the church and from the career of Paul that Gentile Christianity emerged triumphant, not because of the failure of the church to reach out to the Jews, but because of the rejection of the gospel by the Jews and the overwhelmingly positive reaction of the Gentiles to it.

The narrative ends rather abruptly. Luke simply states that Paul, awaiting trial, lived in Rome two years, boldly proclaiming the kingdom of God and the Lord Jesus Christ without hindrance (28:31). Nothing is said about the outcome of Paul's trial or his life. If, as most scholars agree, Luke wrote long after the death of Paul, why did he not mention these matters that, at least to modern readers, are of great interest? Obviously, no one can answer the question with certainty. Evidently, though, Luke's concerns were not merely biographical. Remember that after the Jerusalem Conference, he never again referred to Peter, although we can assume that he must have known something about Peter's activities. Actually, Luke's story is bigger than that of Peter or Paul. It is bigger than that of any individual local church, whether in Jerusalem or Corinth or Ephesus or Rome. His story is that in spite of overwhelming obstacles, the gospel could not be stopped. God's salvific intention was realized in these early crucial decades because of the unlimited vision of Stephen, Philip, Paul, and others like them who were willing to defy racial, religious, cultural, and geographical boundaries to proclaim the good news to all who would listen. Triumph came to the church because of the willingness of these to undertake a mission to the Gentiles!

Notes

[1]See Frank Stagg, *The Book of Acts: The Early Struggle for an Unhindered Gospel* (Nashville: Broadman, 1955) 12-17.

[2]Chronology for Paul's life cannot be established with certitude, but in general scholars date Paul's arrival in Macedonia about AD 50 and the writing of Romans in the mid-50s.

[3]See also the unnamed but leading women in Thessalonica (17:4) and Berea (17:12), along with Damaris in Athens (17:34) and Priscilla in Corinth (18:2).

[4]For brief summaries of these philosophies, see these articles by Robert M. Shurden in the *Mercer Dictionary of the Bible* (Macon GA: Mercer University, 1990): "Epicureans" (257-58) and "Stoics" (857-58).

[5]Standard New Testament introductions and Bible dictionaries contain such chronologies. Although all of these start with the data from the Gallio inscription, they vary from each other at other points. Even with the Gallio inscription, there is no universally accepted chronology of the life of Paul.

[6]We will look at this collection ministry from Paul's perspective in the next chapter.

[7]Exceptions are Paul's experiences on Malta (28:1-10) and the summary of his preaching in Rome while awaiting trial (28:30-31).

[8]See John B. Polhill, *Acts*, The New American Commentary, vol. 26 (Nashville: Broadman, 1992) 447.

EPISTLES OF PAUL

Paul, the Missionary

With the exception of Jesus, no one in the history of Christianity has played a more significant role than Paul, apostle extraordinary. This fact has already become apparent to us as we have examined the book of Acts, for more than half of that narrative is devoted to his career. Imagine how truncated Luke's story would have been if he had tried to tell it without mentioning Paul! Furthermore, half of the New Testament writings—thirteen out of twenty-seven—bear his name. In actual bulk, his letters comprise approximately one-fourth of the total New Testament. Only one other writer has contributed more: the author of Luke and Acts.[1] Yet that author is anonymous; we know virtually nothing about him. Paul's documents, by contrast, are thoroughly colored by his personality. We cannot separate his written legacy from his person.

Perhaps even more significant than the quantity of his writings is their age. His letters are our oldest extant Christian literature. From a chronological perspective the present-day arrangement of the documents in the New Testament is somewhat misleading. Since the Gospels are placed first, we tend to think they were written before the remaining books. Obviously, the story they tell chronologically precedes everything else in the New Testament. But Paul wrote his letters long before the Gospels were recorded. Although we cannot state for a fact that he was the first Christian writer, he certainly was the first whose materials have been preserved for us within the New Testament canon.

As Acts has demonstrated, Paul, more than any other individual person, transformed Christianity in those earliest decades from a narrow, nationalistic, Palestinian Jewish sect to an inclusive, worldwide religious movement. Steeped in both Greco-Roman culture and a fervent Jewish piety, he was able to bridge the gap between the two in such a way that he was able, as Davies put it, "to plant a Palestinian gospel in an alien world and yet keep it true to its root."[2]

Through the legacy of his writings, furthermore, Paul has continued to have a formidable impact on subsequent Christian history. Augustine, the great fourth-century church leader and the most significant theologian (after Paul) of the ancient church, turned from a life of debauchery to the Christian faith upon reading Romans 13:13-14. A thousand years later Martin Luther ushered in the Protestant Reformation, primarily as a result of insights gained from his intensive study of the Pauline epistles.

Further, two centuries later John Wesley's heart was "strangely warmed" as he heard someone reading from Luther's Preface to the Epistle to the Romans; thereby began the Methodist movement and the evangelical revival of the eighteenth century. Finally, Karl Barth, arguably the most significant theologian of the twentieth century, rose to prominence as a result of his study of Paul and the publication of his commentary on Romans. From the first century to the present, Paul has been associated with the most vibrant movements in the life of the church.

As we began our survey of Acts, we noted many unique features of the book. Now as we begin our study of Paul, we see that he, too, was unique. Not only was he the innovator in writing Christian documents, but also he wrote more individual New Testament documents than any other person. Furthermore, in the history of Christianity his documents uniquely served as catalysts that provoked the actions of these important individuals mentioned earlier and the movements they began. Moreover, as Acts shows, Paul's role in the expansion of early Christianity was singularly significant. Although he had traveling companions who were with him from time to time, although he was not hesitant to recognize others as his co-laborers, although others also proclaimed the gospel, he is the figure who stands out in the Acts story. He was a unique missionary.

I would like to begin our overview of Paul's letters by picking up on the role of missionary that dominates Luke's presentation in Acts. In the remaining chapters, then, we will concentrate on his roles as theologian and pastor. Traditionally, Christians have assumed that to understand Paul's thought, one should examine his letters; but to know about his life, one should rely upon the book of Acts. Certainly, as we explore Paul's theology and pastoral concerns, we will look closely at what he wrote. What about his career as a missionary? Do we only look at Acts?

The Letters as Sources for a Life of Paul

Two sources for studying the life of Paul are available: the book of Acts and autobiographical comments Paul makes in his own writings. The two sources are quite different in both purpose and genre. On the one hand, Paul's letters were not intended to be autobiographies; they were letters dealing with specific matters of concern to specific churches or individuals. Occasionally in these missives, Paul makes incidental comments about his own personal circumstances. Acts, on the other hand, was written as a narrative moving chronologically from one incident to another with much of the material dealing with biographical data about Paul. Even so, we must remember that Luke was giving a theological interpretation of history; and though he centered his story around particular personalities, biography was not his primary concern.

Sometimes when the two sources deal with the same incident, they differ in some details. We have already seen an example of this in the two accounts of the Jerusalem Conference, one from Acts 15 and the other from Galatians 2. At times one source is silent about a matter described in the other. Luke, for example, relates Paul's experiences in the founding of the church at Philippi. Yet, Paul in an intimate letter to that congregation never refers to that period of beginnings. In turn, Paul records in detail his rationale and plans for taking the collection among the Gentile churches for the benefit of the poor Christians in Jerusalem, while Luke makes virtually no reference to this endeavor.

In trying to make sense of these differences in the source materials, modern scholars have assessed the evidence in different ways. One has been to take Acts at face value as a historical source and to force details from the letters into appropriate points in the Lukan outline of Paul's career. Scholars pursuing this approach often have not fully appreciated the theological nature of Acts, failing to realize that biography is not Luke's primary goal.

Another is practically to disregard Acts as a legitimate source altogether. Those who take this tact take the theological nature of the document so seriously that they are skeptical about virtually every historical detail. For these, the only reliable information must be gained from the letters. Yet, these scholars fail to see that autobiographical statements are not always objective reflections of simple, hard facts. Such memories are often slanted by the biases and perspectives of the one who shares them.

Perhaps the best approach is to find value in both sources, recognizing that the materials from Paul are primary and that data from Acts may offer valuable supplementary information. When the two sources differ, scholars who take this approach give deference to Paul, but they do not totally dismiss Acts. They recognize that there are too many places where the two correspond for one to disregard totally the information in Acts. When one compares the similarities in Acts and the Epistles, it becomes quite obvious that the author of Acts actually knew quite a bit about Paul.[3] By relying on the letters as primary and inserting from Acts other appropriate material that does not conflict with the epistolary material, these scholars achieve a balanced and reliable understanding of Paul. I assume this approach as we now begin to seek an understanding of Paul the missionary.

Paul's Strategy

Not only was Paul an innovator as a Christian author, but he was also an innovator as a missionary. He was not an innovator, however, in the preaching of the gospel; Peter, among others, preceded him in this effort. Nor was he the first to travel to a new region with the Christian message. Philip had gone to Samaria, and other unnamed Hellenists had reached Phoenicia, Cyprus, and Antioch (Acts 11:19-20). These persons, however, had not gone to these places motivated by a desire to preach the gospel; they traveled so that they might escape persecution in Jerusalem, and they preached as they went. By contrast, the Acts account indicates that Paul, with Barnabas, was the first to go places in order to preach the gospel (chaps. 13–14). This missionary team was not fleeing from Antioch; they intentionally decided to go to Cyprus and Asia Minor. According to Acts, a missionary journey deliberately undertaken to proclaim the gospel in new territories was the innovation of Paul and Barnabas, the first missionary team.

But was the so-called "first missionary journey" of Acts 13–14 the first missionary journey of Paul? Clues in Paul's letters indicate it was not. In his own account of his conversion experience (Gal 3:13-24) Paul narrates this sequence of events:

- God revealed His Son to Paul so that he might proclaim Christ among the Gentiles.
- Paul did not confer with others, particularly those in Jerusalem who were apostles before him.
- Paul went away to Arabia and at some point returned to Damascus.
- After three years Paul finally made a "get-acquainted visit" with Peter and James in Jerusalem.

Implied in the text is that the activity in Arabia—about which Acts is silent—and Damascus spanned three years. What was Paul doing during this time? Many commentators, perhaps envisioning a desert scene, have speculated that Paul went to

Arabia for a period of contemplation, a time of withdrawal for communion with God, and then returned to Damascus where he preached in the synagogues (Acts 9:20). Two comments from Paul, however, suggest that, more than likely, Paul was in Arabia preaching the gospel.

First, in this passage from Galatians Paul is asserting his independence from the Jerusalem leaders. Therefore, for him to note that his sojourn in Arabia immediately followed his call to go to the Gentiles, probably indicates that he started fulfilling his call even before he met the leaders in Jerusalem; his ministry was independent of any influence from them.

Second, in 2 Corinthians 11:32 Paul indicates he had to escape from Damascus, not to get away from the Jews (so, Acts 9:23) but from the governor under King Aretas of Nabatea (Arabia). Would this representative of Aretas have plotted against Paul because he was meditating in Arabia? Or, more likely, did the opposition to Paul arise from his preaching in that area? If Paul was involved in a preaching mission in Arabia, which seems most likely, his innovative missionary activity preceded by years the journey described in Acts 13–14.

Intentional travel from place to place to proclaim the gospel was definitely a part of Paul's strategy for fulfilling his apostolic call. By looking at the letters and Acts, can we detect other elements of that strategy?

Where Did Paul Go?

Other than the statement in Galatians 1:21 that he had gone into the regions of Syria and Cilicia, autobiographical comments by Paul about places or incidents that parallel the Acts version of the first missionary campaign do not exist. Since Paul mentions in the following verses (2:1ff.) his going to Jerusalem to lay before the congregation the gospel he had proclaimed among the Gentiles (the Jerusalem Conference), we can conclude from his account that he had already been active in preaching the gospel to non-Jews. Galatians, though, is not explicit about where this activity had taken place. Here, then, the Acts account is instructive, for it presents a specific itinerary, and that itinerary does not conflict with any information from the letters.

The pattern of Paul's first mission effort in Acts follows a typical journey motif. Paul and Barnabas traveled from one end of Cyprus to the other before sailing to Asia Minor. After docking in Attalia, they moved in succession to Perga, Antioch, Iconium, Lystra, and Derbe from which they basically retraced their steps to Syrian Antioch. The length of the visit to any one city was relatively short, perhaps because of the opposition they encountered in these various places. When such obstacles arose, the team simply moved on to another location to continue their ministry there. The new place apparently was dictated by the direction the road followed rather by than the deliberate choice of the missionary team. Earlier, Cyprus evidently had been visited by design, for Barnabas was a native of the island. By contrast, instead of having a predetermined itinerary when they got to Asia Minor, the team seems to have gone wherever the road happened to lead.

One possible exception to this pattern is found at the end of this sojourn. At Derbe, Paul, ready to return to Syria, did not continue to travel south and east on the available roads in order to reach Syrian Antioch. Rather, at risk to his own life, he returned to the cities where he had just established fledgling Christian communities. Moreover, after the Jerusalem Conference, the impetus for starting the second mission came from Paul's desire to revisit these churches once again (Acts 15:36). Not only did he check on the young Christian communities at the beginning of this new venture (15:41–16:1), but also between his lengthy stays in Corinth and Ephesus he made it a point to visit these communities yet another time to strengthen the Christians there (18:23). Apparently, the repeat visit to encourage young Christians became an element of Paul's strategy. Further evidence of this pattern was the return to Macedonia and Achaia at the end of the Aegean mission (Acts 20:1-2; cf. Rom 15:26, which implies that Paul had returned to these regions).

Overall, the initial mission in Asia Minor seems to have lacked a precise geographical plan. The account of the Aegean mission, however, reflects a more deliberate itinerary, even though Paul was not always able to follow it. To begin with, the trip was initiated by Paul's desire to revisit the churches established on the previous mission. Further, Paul evidently had intended to go into the province of Asia, but he was prevented from doing so in some way by the Holy Spirit. Instead, he went to Phrygia and Galatia (Acts 16:6). In Galatians 4:13 Paul indicates that he first preached to the readers because of a bodily ailment; perhaps this malady provided the occasion for reflection in which he perceived divine negation of his plans. Likewise, he had also intended to enter Bithynia, but again was prevented by the Spirit (Acts 16:7). Although Paul seems to have had a plan, he was flexible enough to make adaptations when external circumstances or his perception of the will of God dictated.

After the Macedonian vision led him to European soil, another aspect of his overall plan of action emerged. Concentrating on Philippi, Thessalonica, Athens, Corinth, and then Ephesus, Paul demonstrated a deliberate pattern of establishing churches in the major cities, rather than trying to evangelize whole districts as he had in Asia Minor. From these congregations the gospel could be carried by others along trade routes into the smaller towns of the surrounding territories. In fact, shifting from a rather itinerant ministry to one of settling in major metropolitan areas such as Corinth and Ephesus allowed Paul the opportunity to organize mission forays by his associates into outlying regions. The Letter to the Colossians assumes such a situation, for in this letter Paul wrote to a church he had not founded and had never visited (2:1), but for whom he felt a sense of pastoral responsibility (1:24-26). These Christians living about 110 miles east of Ephesus had first heard of Christ from Epaphras (1:7), one of Paul's colleagues who had also ministered in the neighboring towns of Laodicea and Hierapolis (4:12-13) and who was now with Paul as he wrote.

On a more practical level, the major cities probably were also fiscally advantageous for Paul, for in them he could have more opportunity for making a living. In Corinth, according to Acts 18:3, Paul worked with Aquila at their common trade, tentmaking. Traditionally, the term for this craft has been interpreted as working with goat hair fabric, one of the products of Paul's native Cilicia, but it could have a broader meaning of leather worker. More significant than the exact nature of his work is the fact that in Corinth, Paul was engaged in a secular occupation while he spread the gospel. In modern terms, he was bi-vocational. Realistically, the pattern at Corinth was probably characteristic of his entire missionary career. Not only is this affirmed in Acts (see 20:33-35), but also in 1 Thessalonians 2:9 and 1 Corinthians 9:14-15. Paul supported himself, for he did want not to be a financial burden for those to whom he was ministering. He did accept gifts from churches where he was no longer working (2 Cor 11:9; Phil 4:15-16); but apparently from whatever church he currently served, he expected and accepted no remuneration.

One final element in the geographical aspect of Paul's missionary strategy remains. Paul liked to establish new work in areas where the gospel had not yet been proclaimed (Rom 15:20). Again to use modern terms, Paul evidently was a "church-planter," one whose gifts were amenable to starting new churches. When the work in an area was firmly established, he felt comfortable in leaving it with others to lead while he moved on to new territory. This pattern is seen not only in Acts as Paul leaves Ephesus (19:21), but it is also confirmed by statements in Romans where Paul indicates that his work in the Aegean area is finished and he anticipates a mission to Spain (15:23-24).

What Did Paul Do?

Upon reading Acts, one's initial impression is that preaching was Paul's primary activity in his missionary treks. The examples of sermons to the Jews in Antioch (ch. 13) and to the pagans in Athens (ch. 17) suggest that Paul was an itinerant preacher, proclaiming the message about Jesus from day to day to whomever he encountered wherever he went. At least a part of this picture was called into question by scholars of an earlier generation who questioned Paul's engagement with Jews. They interpreted at face value Paul's words about an agreement reached at the Jerusalem Conference that he would minister to the Gentiles while the Jerusalem leaders would minister to the Jews (Gal 2:9). Thus, these interpreters tended to dismiss any of the Acts materials that even hint at Paul's outreach to the Jews.

Yet, in 2 Corinthians 11:23-28 where Paul lists hardships he had endured for the cause of Christ, he mentions that on five different occasions he had received the "forty lashes minus one," a typical Jewish punishment inflicted by the synagogues (v. 24). Why would he have undergone such treatment by the Jews unless he had gone to the synagogues and approached those congregations with his proclamation of Jesus Christ? Surely he had some contact or relationship with the synagogues if they subjected him to corporal punishment. The fact that Paul had been called to be an apostle to the Gentiles did not prevent him from preaching to Jews also. In fact, the habit of seeking out the synagogues in each new city, as Acts describes Paul's procedure, was certainly logical. The Jews and the God-fearers attached to them provided Paul with the audience best prepared to hear his message; they already believed in the monotheistic God who Paul proclaimed had made himself manifest in Jesus. Furthermore, in his theological scheme of salvation, the gospel was for the Jew first and also for the Greek (Rom 1:16); he would not have failed to preach to Jews when he had opportunity.

The typical failure of the Jews to respond, however, did not throw him into despair. When one door was closed to Paul, he searched for another that was open. When he was rejected in the synagogues, he turned to the Gentiles. At best the ministry in the synagogue was temporary. It was a good place to begin, but it was not a place to which Paul's ministry could have been confined. Distinctive Christian practices such as baptism and the Lord's Supper were inappropriate for the synagogue setting.

Contrary to the impression from Acts, Paul's public preaching might not have been the primary setting in which he communicated the Christian message. After all, he acknowledged his opponents' accusation that he had an unimpressive physical presence and speaking ability (2 Cor 10:10). From hints in the letters it appears he was not a street corner preacher, spending his days trying to attract a crowd. In the passages we have just examined we see that Paul was engaged in a secular occupation in order to earn his livelihood. More than likely, Paul shared the gospel as he worked in the marketplace. Typical commercial buildings provided both dwelling places on upper floors and first-level shops that opened into the streets. In Corinth, for example, Paul likely shared living quarters with Aquila and Priscilla in one of the upstairs apartments while they maintained a shop for production and sales of their wares below. As he worked on the animal skins, he engaged customers and others walking through the marketplace and passing by the open end of the shop. Evangelism was based more on a one-on-one type of encounter rather than the public proclamation of the good news. In the light of the Acts presentation, there is no reason to doubt that from time to time he did preach in synagogues, public halls, and even open-air settings. The bulk of his work, however, was probably accomplished as he plied his trade.

As we have already seen, another significant activity in Paul's missionary strategy was revisiting churches where he had formerly served. What if circumstances prevented those return visits? Then Paul reverted to writing letters that could be delivered to these congregations. Ironically, we know Paul best for the letters he wrote; yet, for all practical purposes, the letters were substitutes for the visits he preferred to make. Since the letters have emerged as such a significant accomplishment of his career, we will treat them in a separate category.

To complete our understanding of the kinds of things Paul did as a missionary, we must look at one other major undertaking: the collection of money from his Gentile churches for the poor among the saints in Jerusalem. Throughout Paul's ministry a sharp division existed within first-century Christianity. To use a modern term, there were virtually two "denominations": Jewish Christianity and Gentile Christianity. For Paul who saw the church as the body of Christ (1 Cor 12:14-31), an entity in which no disunity or lack of harmony should be present, the division was deplorable. Always seeking to reconcile those who were estranged from others within the church, Paul devised a plan to promote harmony between the two factions. What better way to unite alienated parties than to foster a feeling of mutual dependence, to make each feel indebted to the other? Obviously, Gentile Christians were obligated to the Jewish Christians, for through these Jewish believers the Gentiles had been brought to Christ. How, though, could he create an awareness of indebtedness on the part of the Jewish Christians to the Gentiles? He found the answer in one word: money.

Acts indicates that many of the Jewish Christians were impoverished. The controversy between Hebrews and Hellenists emerged from the daily distribution of food to the indigent widows (6:1). Later, because of famine, a relief offering was sent by the church at Antioch to needy fellow believers in Jerusalem (11:29-30). Further, in Paul's account of the conclusion of the Jerusalem Conference he indicates he was admonished by the Jerusalem leaders to remember the poor, probably those in Jerusalem. This, he says, he was eager to do (Gal 2:10). Thus towards the end of the Aegean mission, Paul decided to collect money from the various Gentile churches to send to Jerusalem. If the Gentile Christians sent money to their Jewish brothers and sisters who were in need, perhaps then the Jewish Christians would feel indebted to the Gentiles. With a recognized mutual dependency, they could resolve their differences, and unity could be achieved. So important was the collection to Paul, he postponed indefinitely his plans for taking the gospel west to Spain so that he could gather the funds and take them east to Jerusalem.

Encouragement and actual instructions for the collecting of these funds are found in 1 Corinthians 16:1-4 and 2 Corinthians 8:1-9:15. Moreover, in Romans 15:25-29 Paul explains to his readers his rationale for this undertaking when he asks for their prayer support as he takes the offering to Jerusalem (15:30-32). Attention is given to this enterprise in Paul's three longest letters!

Ironically, though, Acts makes no mention of this endeavor.[4] After completing his work in Ephesus, the Lukan Paul retraces his steps around the Aegean to Macedonia and Achaia (20:2-3), but the reason for this journey is not explicitly stated. Included in the Pauline references are comments about the representatives who were to be chosen to escort Paul and the gift (1 Cor 16:3-4), but in none of these three letters are any of the representatives named. In Acts, however, representatives from the various churches who accompanied Paul to Jerusalem are listed, even though the offering they bring is not.

Further, Luke unintentionally gives us more information about the participants in this undertaking than Paul himself does. He not only lists their names, but he also indicates the home churches of these individuals. In fact, Luke suggests a wider participation in the collection than is intimated in the letters. Paul mentions Galatia, Macedonia, and Achaia (1 Cor 16:2; Rom 15:26), while Luke also lists representatives from Asia (Acts 20:4-5). In fact, Trophimus, a member of the Asian delegation, is the person whose presence with Paul in the temple sparks the riot leading to Paul's arrest (21:29).

Why does Acts not specifically mention the collection? Luke knew about Paul's final journey to Jerusalem; he knew that Paul, instead of traveling directly from Ephesus to Jerusalem, had retraced his steps around the Aegean just before this eventful journey; he knew that Paul had taken representatives of various Gentile churches with him. Did he simply not know about the collection? I doubt it. It seems to me that Luke omitted reference to the offering because the collection was unsuccessful; it did not achieve the goal Paul desired.[5] Remember, Luke was selective in what he recorded; here I think he simply chose not to describe an effort of Paul that turned out to be futile.

The collection does show Paul's concern for a practical, rather than theoretical, Christianity. Paul did not simply proclaim a reconciling gospel; by his collection ministry he endeavored to facilitate reconciliation between the two great branches of Christianity.

With Whom Did Paul Serve?

Paul was not a loner. In the Acts accounts he rarely undertook his missionary ventures by himself.[6] Instead he had partners or companions who accompanied him along the way—Barnabas and John Mark in the first mission; Silas and Timothy in the Aegean mission. Likewise in his correspondence he frequently mentions his co-workers. Frequently he uses Greek nouns compounded with the preposition *syn* (together, with) to describe these who labored with him; for example, he mentions fourteen fellow workers, four fellow prisoners, two fellow soldiers, and two fellow slaves. He did not consider these people to be underlings or lackeys; they were colleagues and partners who shared the tasks with him.

As Paul proclaimed Christ, he made both fast friends and fierce foes. People were not indifferent to him, for they either loved him or hated him. Paul's writings definitely depict bitter controversies with those who tried to undermine his work, the Judaizers in Galatia and the superlative apostles in Corinth, for examples. Yet at the end of his letters the long lists of folk to whom he sends personal greetings indicate warm relationships he enjoyed with people in the churches.[7]

Friendship is a two-way street; it implies a mutual reliance and dependence. Obviously these people felt a dependency upon Paul, but he also felt a reliance upon them. Some of these such as Aquila and Priscilla (Rom 16:3) and Epaphroditus (Phil 2:30) even risked their own lives for the sake of his. Paul had the ability to make people feel they were as important to him as he was to them (Rom 1:11-12; 1 Cor 16:17-18). Certainly his co-workers and friends contributed to the success of his mission.

The Letters and the Pauline Mission

Although we have mentioned the letters of Paul in several contexts, we must now turn to them for a more deliberate overview of their nature and function within Paul's ministry. Then in the next two chapters we will get an overview of their content.

For many modern Christians, perhaps the best known fact about Paul is that he wrote many of the books of the New Testament. When Paul wrote, however, he had no awareness that he was writing Scripture. Rather, he was writing letters to churches and individuals for whom he was concerned but whom for various reasons he could not at that time visit.[8] The form he used was typically Greco-Roman and quite different from ours. The first word in his letters, for example, is "Paul." In his culture the name of the sender was always listed first. Because letters were written on scrolls, it was quite convenient to have the sender identified at the beginning rather than at the end as we usually do. The pattern for Paul's letters, then, is as follows:

• Paul's name and sometimes the names of his companions
• the name of the recipients
• a salutation
• a prayer of thanksgiving for the readers
• the body
• the conclusion, which often includes personal greetings

Even though he used the customary form of his day, Paul infused the elements of that form with Christian meaning. Let me give one example. A typical Greco-Roman salutation was "Greetings" (Greek *chairein*). Paul never uses this term, but in its place he uses "Grace" (Greek *charis*), a cognate of the Greek greeting, but also a term central to his theology, for it connotes the idea of God's free gift. Moreover, always coupled with "Grace" in Paul's opening words is "Peace" (Hebrew *shalom*), the typical Jewish greeting. The terms are always in the same order: grace and peace, not peace and grace. For Paul, only those who have experienced God's grace can know real peace.

Paul typically dictated his letters. Perhaps in part he did this because of bad eyesight, for in Galatians 6:11, where he apparently took the pen from the scribe, he remarks about the large letters with which he writes. In 2 Thessalonians 3:17 Paul again signed a personal greeting, this time noting his distinctive handwriting. Did he write with large letters because he did not see well? If so, dictating letters would be of great benefit, for a scribe could write legibly in much less space than Paul. Additional comments about his writing a greeting with his own hand are found in 1 Corinthians 16:21 and Colossians 4:18; and in Romans 16:22 Tertius, the scribe who actually penned the letter, identifies himself.

Two methods of dictation were employed in the first century. First, a sender could dictate word for word what was to be recorded by the secretary. Second, the general idea of what the sender intended could be indicated to the scribe who then had great latitude to verbalize the ideas and to impose his style and phraseology on the finished letter. In the latter method the secretary actually functioned somewhat as a co-author. Which method Paul used we cannot determine with certainty, although similarities in style and vocabulary in his major letters tend to support the verbal dictation method. Of course, these similarities could also be attributed to the same secretary. Perhaps he utilized both, stating his own words precisely in some letters and allowing the secretary some creativity in others.

With the exception of personal notes such as Philemon, Paul's writings were intended to be read aloud before the congregations to whom they were addressed (1 Thess 5:27). Thus the language is appropriately more formal than what might be found in a casual exchange between friends. Therefore, some scholars prefer the term "epistles" to "letters" as a reminder of the more formal nature of these documents.

The letters addressed very specific issues for specific people in a specific place at a specific time. They were occasional, written for a particular occasion. At times Paul wrote in response to a letter he had received from a church (1 Cor 7:1). At other times he wrote in response to what he had heard about the church (1 Thess 3:6). In every case the letter was intended to address a particular matter of importance to Paul and/or the readers at that moment. Since the letters are bound together for us in one volume, we sometimes miss the individuality of the letter or the response Paul is making to a particular church. We treat them all as Scripture, each standing on equal footing with the others. But they would not have been seen that way by the original recipients. If letters had been crossed in the "mail," those first readers would have been confused. To the Corinthians Paul wrote some very pointed ethical advice about matters relevant to them, such as the problem of a man sleeping with his stepmother (1 Cor 5:1). To the Philippians he wrote to thank them for a financial gift they had sent and to allay their concerns about their member Epaphroditus who fell seriously ill after bringing the money to Paul. Imagine the perplexity for the readers if somehow the Philippians received the letter to the Corinthians and vice versa. The Philippians did not have a problem of incest within the church, and the Corinthians did not even know Epaphroditus!

Our understanding of the letters, therefore, is facilitated by our understanding of the occasion. Unfortunately, we cannot always reconstruct the complete set of circumstances that prompted a letter. We have only Paul's responses from which we must deduce the questions and perspectives of those to whom he wrote. In a sense, reading the letters is similar to listening to one side of a phone conversation; we do not know precisely what the other party has said, but we can reasonably reconstruct it from what we do hear. That we cannot know all of the circumstances is easily demonstrated by efforts to establish the dates of the letters. Generally, scholars agree that Paul's writing career extended over one decade, from the early 50s to the early 60s. Beyond these general parameters, though, there is no semblance of unity in scholars' minds about the precise date of each document. For that matter, specialists in the study of Paul do not even agree about the correct sequence of the letters! Often present-day readers inaccurately assume that the canonical order of the individual writings is also their chronological order. Paul's letters, however, are arranged by length. Actually, two groupings of Paul's letters are included in the New Testament: the first nine are addressed to churches; the last four are addressed to individuals. Within each group the arrangement moves from the longest book first to the shortest in last position.

Not all of Paul's letters have been preserved. Paul, for instance, mentions in what we know as 1 Corinthians that he had written an earlier message to that congregation (5:9) Some have tried to identify at least a part of this "previous letter" with a passage in 2 Corinthians 6:14-7:1, but again scholars are divided about this identification. Likewise, mention of a severe letter (2 Cor 7:8) and a Laodicean letter (Col 4:16) apparently refer to individual documents we no longer have.

On the other hand, many scholars feel that not all of the Pauline letters that have been preserved in the New Testament were actually written by Paul. Because of language and style, theology, the historical situation that is assumed, or church organization that is understood within some of the letters, the Pauline authorship of at least six of the thirteen letters has sometimes been questioned. Generally, those who take such a position do not suggest that these writings are fraudulent or forgeries. Instead, they suggest that after the death of Paul one of his close associates or disciples, who considered himself an authoritative interpreter of the apostle, penned a letter under his name to express Paul's thoughts to the disciple's contemporary situation. In this sense the letter was an attempt to continue Paul's work; Paul's name was used to indicate the authority behind the letter. To be fair, I must point out that those taking such a position do not necessarily dispute the scriptural authority of these letters; they are not trying to remove them from the canon. They simply suggest that the actual authors of the documents are unknown.

Obviously, not all scholars agree with this position. Many take the name of the sender at face value, assuming that if the letter claims to have been written by Paul, it must have been. I would be less than frank, though, if I did not admit that scholarship is divided over the issue. Seven of Paul's letters are uncontested. There is no serious scholarly doubt that Paul wrote Romans, 1 Corinthians, 2 Corinthians, Galatians, Philippians, 1 Thessalonians, and Philemon. Roughly evenly divided are the scholars who accept and those who deny the Pauline authorship of 2 Thessalonians and Colossians. A significant majority question Ephesians and the Pastoral Letters (1 and 2 Timothy and Titus). Examination of the issues related to each of these is beyond the scope of our study, but standard New Testament introductions, Bible dictionaries, and commentaries present the various positions.[9]

Paul, the Man and His Mission

Paul was not much to look at. Both his physical presence and his speaking ability were unimpressive. He was not a man of wealth. In his Greco-Roman world he was a member of an ethnic minority. Though Acts notes he was a Roman citizen, he was not socially prominent in that society. In a sense he was a vagabond, traveling from one place to another carrying his worldly possessions in a knapsack on his back. In his travels he probably covered more than 3,500 miles, most of the trip made on foot over rigorous terrain, some of it by sea in less than ideal conditions. He was trained as a tentmaker, and he had to find work as he moved from town to town to supply his basic necessities. Other than a sister and nephew in Jerusalem, he had no family. Everywhere he went he was able to make friends who were intensely loyal to him; but he also found himself at odds with many, many more. Prone to illness, he suffered some physical malady that to him was a "thorn in the flesh" (2 Cor 12:7).

In his own words he suffered innumerable hardships: repeated scourgings with whips and beatings with rods, stoning, multiple shipwrecks, dangers on land and sea, hardships in the cities and open country, sleep deprivation, hunger, thirst, inadequate clothing, and exposure to the cold (11:23-27). But he would not quit.

> I am content with weaknesses, insults, hardships, persecutions, and calamities for the sake of Christ. (12:10)

> I have learned to be content with whatever I have. I know what it is to have little, and I know what it is to have plenty. In any and all circumstances I have learned the secret of being well-fed and of going hungry, of having plenty and of being in need. I can do all things through him who strengthens me. (Phil 4:11b-13)

For Paul, the hardships were irrelevant. He was a man transformed by an encounter with the risen Christ and obsessed with sharing the love of Christ with people throughout his world. He left a legacy that has been unsurpassed.

Notes

[1]Raymond E. Brown, *An Introduction to the New Testament*, The Anchor Bible Reference Library (New York: Doubleday, 1997) 451, calculates the total number of words in Paul's letters at 32,350, while Luke-Acts contains 37,800. At random I picked one of the English Bibles from my shelf and discovered that of the 258 pages in the New Testament, 64 were required to print Paul's letters, while Luke-Acts needed 69.

[2]W. D. Davies, "The Apostolic Age and the Life of Paul," *Peake's Commentary on the Bible* (New York: Thomas Nelson, 1962) 878.

[3]An excellent example of a such a comparison is found in Brown, 424, who gives a table that outlines in parallel fashion the activities of Paul in the two sources.

[4]One possible exception may be a passing reference in one of Paul's defenses after his arrest in the temple (Acts 24:17).

[5]The collection is not the only material Luke purposely omitted. In 2 Cor 2:1 Paul indicates that he does not want to make another "painful" visit to the church at Corinth, and later in 13:1 he indicates he is getting ready to visit them for the third time. Luke, however, mentions only two visits to Corinth (18:1; 20:2), neither of which could be deemed "painful." Again I conclude that

Luke omitted the middle visit, the painful one, because it was a failure. Paul had gone in order to be reconciled to the Corinthians who at that time were estranged from him. But the results were far from satisfactory; actually, the quick trip from Ephesus to Corinth had further alienated the Corinthians.

[6]The experience in Athens (Acts 17) is a notable exception.

[7]See especially Rom 16:3-16 where he mentions more than twenty-five individuals.

[8]In four letters, for example, Paul indicates he is in prison at the time he writes (Phil 1:12-13; Phlm 1; Col 4:10, 18; Eph 3:1; 4:1).

[9]A particularly informative discussion of the issue in general is found in Brown, 585-89. Although Brown accepts in principle that some of these writings are not actually by Paul, he notes difficulties that must be kept in mind by each reader who seriously grapples with this issue.

Paul, the Theologian

As Paul moved from place to place in his missionary ventures, problems often arose in the churches he had left behind, for example, uncertainty about their Christian beliefs or confusion about their Christian behavior. Often these churches sent messages to Paul asking for his advice, and sporadically Paul heard reports about difficulties in a particular congregation. When he received these requests and reports, Paul typically responded by writing letters intended to explain and to encourage, to comfort and to correct. His answers and admonitions have influenced Christian faith and practice ever since.

In this chapter we will sample some of the responses he made about matters of Christian belief; in other words, we will look in cursory fashion at Paul's theology. To some extent, the term "theology" in this context is somewhat misleading. Paul, technically, was not a "theologian"; that is, Paul never set out to compile or to sort his Christian convictions into an organized system of belief. He was not a theorist; he was a practical missionary-pastor who responded to particular people at a particular time about particular issues of concern. To be sure, his responses were based on his theological reflections and understandings. But when we look at any specific passage in one of his letters, we must always remember that he was responding to a particular situation or question and not lifting a subpoint from a fully outlined theological system.

A good example of a situational response is found in his earliest letter, 1 Thessalonians. Soon after departing from the church at Thessalonica, Paul sent Timothy and Silvanus (known as Silas in Acts) back to check on the young congregation as he went on to Athens alone. When they joined him in Corinth with reports about the church, he sent this letter. Obviously, one of the theological concerns bothering the church concerned the return of Christ. Specifically, the Thessalonians wanted to know if Christians who had died prior to the return would participate in the event. Although specific details related to the question are not spelled out in the letter—remember, we are hearing just one side of a "phone conversation"—it is probable that a death had occurred within the congregation. Their concern was not abstract; it was personal. What would be the status of this loved one when Christ comes back? Will only those who are alive at the time of Christ's return be able to participate in it?

The immediacy of their concern sometimes evades us who live two thousand years later than they. We have lost the sense of expectancy of those early Christians who fervently believed that Christ was on the verge of returning at any moment. Notice in Paul's response, for example, his expectation that he will be alive at the return: "We who are alive, who are left until the coming of the Lord, will by no means precede those who have died" (4:15). In order to understand their concern, then, we must not forget they were the first generation of Christians; they did not have the experience of others to build upon.

To reassure his readers, Paul answers their question *three* times in this one brief passage: God will bring with Jesus the ones who are dead (v. 14); those who are alive will not precede the ones who are dead (v. 15); and Christians who have died will rise first (v. 16). Paul's message is straightforward: yes, the dead will participate; in fact, they will be involved before we are! Please notice what Paul does not say. He does not mention what happens to the dead who are not Christians, nor does he specify what happens to the living who do not belong to Christ. He does not mention judgment, the nature of the resurrection body, heaven, or hell. In other words, he is not giving a carefully outlined theological exposition of the doctrine of the return of Christ. Instead he is answering one, and *only one*, question: will the dead participate?

I wonder if sometimes we do a disservice to Paul and the other New Testament writers when we take a verse dealing with one aspect of an issue from one text and a verse about another aspect from a different text and try to force them into a nice, neat outline on that topic. When I first started teaching many years ago, I had a student who had an amazing chart stretching from wall to wall in his room that gave in sequential order all the events he anticipated would take place before, during, and after the return of Christ. Listed with each event was the scriptural passage that suggested it. Included was this passage from Thessalonians along with other texts from both the Old and New Testaments!

I do not think Paul had such a chart. I am not sure he was ever concerned to systematize all his beliefs about this specific issue. Instead, as problems and questions arose within particular congregations, Paul answered those questions and addressed those problems without trying to explain the relationship of these ideas with those he had discussed in letters to other churches. Paul was not that type of theologian.

From another perspective, though, Paul was very much a theologian. He was one who thought and shared his ideas about matters divine: God, Christ, Spirit, human beings, sin, salvation, the church, the end. The thoughts he expressed in his letters have in turn provided the raw materials for theology that have occupied Christian thinkers for the last two thousand years.

In our overview of the theological matters about which Paul wrote, we cannot possibly deal with every topic. To gain some perspective about his thinking, though, perhaps the best place to start is with Romans, his longest and probably most profound letter. Ironically, after downplaying the idea that he was a systematic theologian, I now have to admit that Romans contains the best organized presentation of his theology.

The circumstances surrounding the letter explain the nature of its contents. Paul did not write to the Romans because he had received theological questions from them that he needed to answer. As a whole, the church in Rome did not even know Paul. He had not founded the church. He had never visited there. The church was significant because it was located in the capital of the empire. Paul was probably in Corinth making the final preparations for his visit to Jerusalem to deliver the money that the Gentile Christians had collected for the poor among the saints in Jerusalem. After delivering this relief offering, Paul hoped to begin a mission to Spain, and he hoped to come by and visit the Romans on his way (Rom 15:23-29).

Uncertain about the way the Gentiles' gift might be received, he asks the Romans to pray for this ministry as he delivers the collection in Jerusalem (vv. 30-31). He also hints that he would like for the Romans to give him financial support as he goes on his way to Spain (v. 24). Paul, then, is asking for prayers and financial provision for his mission to Spain from people who do not know him. What better way to establish rapport with these people than to set down in somewhat systematic fashion the key aspects of the gospel he proclaimed, to show that the message he preached was indeed the essence of what they believed, to demonstrate how much he and they had in common? After the Romans read this presentation, he hoped, they would be able to identify with him and therefore be willing to respond to the requests that he was making.

The first half of Romans, then, contains this presentation of Paul's beliefs.[1] Although this material is the most systematic presentation of his thought to be found in any of his letters, it is not a summary of his complete theology. For example, the Lord's Supper is of special importance to Paul, as is obvious by his comments in 1 Corinthians (10:14-22; 11:17-34). Yet, he does not even mention the Supper in Romans! He has not tried to tell everything, but he has described the foundational beliefs that have shaped his faith.

Justification by Faith

Central to Paul's theology is the idea many students of the Bible have seen as the theme of this letter: justification by faith. Before we look in detail at Paul's theological digest, we should explore the terms in this phrase that he places as a summary statement or heading for all that follows in his discussion (Rom 1:16-17).

Whenever we read the words "justification" and "righteousness" in our English Bibles, we are looking at alternate English translations for one Greek word. It is a term that can legitimately be translated both ways. The same dual translation occurs for the verb and adjective cognates of this noun. "To justify is to make righteous"; one who is "justified" (or "just") is one who is "righteous." Here in 1:17 the idea is first used in reference to God. Righteousness here is an attribute or characteristic of the Deity. In the verbal form, however, it refers to an action of God. God is the one who justifies human beings or makes them righteous. The second use of verse 17 is derived from this verbal understanding. Even though it is used here to describe a human being—the one who is righteous—it actually refers back to the activity of God. One who is righteous (justified) is the one who has been made so by God. For Paul, both an attribute and an action of God are revealed in the gospel.

Many have concentrated on the legal connotations of the translation "justification" to clarify the meaning of the term in Paul's writings, seeing it as metaphor for salvation drawn from the law court. Implied in this interpretation is the idea of acquittal; that is, God declares us innocent even when we are guilty. Although the word took on legal connotations, its root meaning does not have this implication of declaring someone innocent. Originally, it meant to make a person right, not just to call someone right.

One of the features on my computer is the justification of margins. This means I can tell the computer to manipulate the text I am typing so that the first letter of each line is arranged to form a straight margin down the left side of the page, or the last letter of each line to form a straight margin down the right side of the page, or both—for the text on a page to be spaced so that straight margins are found on the left and right sides of the page (like those on this printed page). When I give the command to justify the margins, the computer actually does something to the text; it does not simply call the margins even when they are not. This sense of "justification" is true to the original meaning.

Thus when God justifies a person, God actually makes that person right. The action of making right is God's activity. We cannot achieve this right status on our own.

The second key element in this theme is "faith." Like righteousness, the Greek word here can be translated by more than one English word: "belief," "faith," and "faithfulness." Although the righteousness (both the attribute and the action) of God is revealed in the gospel, it becomes effective for the individual on the basis of faith. In fact, Paul here says that in the gospel God's righteousness is revealed through faith for faith.

Related to this phrase here is another found frequently in Paul's letters about which there has been much recent debate, again because there is more than one way to translate the idea into English: "faith in Jesus" or "the faith of Jesus." Romans 3:21-22 is an example: "But now, apart from the Law, the righteousness of God has been disclosed . . . through faith in Jesus Christ for all who believe." An alternate translation for this statement about faith is "through the faith (faithfulness) of Jesus Christ." Since there is no preposition before the word "Jesus" in the Greek text, either translation is possible.[2] Some interpret these passages to mean the faith or faithfulness of Jesus. The idea could refer to the faith Jesus demonstrated in going to the cross, or it could refer to his faithfulness to God's plan. According to this interpretation, we are justified, made righteous, by *his* faith or faithfulness. The advantage of this position is the total emphasis on the divine aspect of salvation; faith is in no sense a "work" we do to gain salvation, for it is Christ's faith (faithfulness) that makes salvation operable for us.

Others, however, find validity in the traditional translation: faith *in* Jesus. Accordingly, we are justified by our faith in him. Although many verses do not include a preposition preceding "Jesus" (Christ), others include terms that can be translated "in" between "faith" and "Jesus."[3] In these passages the meaning is clarified. Therefore, even though the idea of "faith of Jesus" has much to commend it, these verses with the preposition "in" seem to me to suggest the proper interpretation of those where the preposition is absent. In other words, there are no passages where the idea "faith of Jesus" is unambiguously stated. There are other passages where the idea "faith in Jesus" is clearly present. It seems to me then that we should look to what is clearly stated elsewhere rather than to what is possibly stated to find clues for the proper interpretation of the ambiguous verses. According to this translation, then, is faith something we do, that is, a work, in order to gain salvation? Not at all. In creation God made human beings with the gift of freedom. We are free to choose or to reject God. We are free to believe or to disbelieve, to have faith or not to have faith. From this perspective our faith is in a sense God's gift to us. God has taken the initiative in faith in giving us the capacity for it. Salvation, faith, and grace come from God.

Paul finds in Habakkuk 2:4 scriptural support for his understanding of faith-related righteousness, but with a new emphasis. Traditionally, the Old Testament passage has been translated, "The just shall live by faith." For Paul, though, the truth of the statement is better seen in the idea, "The one who has been justified by faith shall live!" Faith here does not characterize the lifestyle or attitude of one who has been justified; rather faith is the dynamic by which justification becomes operable in a person's life. One who has experienced this transforming experience is the one who will truly live.

The Human Predicament

After setting the theme for his theological presentation, Paul then turns to its development. His first major premise is that all people are in need of this right relationship with God that comes only through faith. In the statement of this theme in Romans 1:16-17 Paul has said that the salvation God offers is available for all people, to the Jew first and also to the Greek. Here he discusses the need of all persons for this salvation, but he reverses the order, talking first about the Gentiles (1:18-32) and then about the Jews (2:1-3:8). Although Paul does not use the word "Gentile" or the word "Greek" as he describes sinful humanity in this first section, he does talk about idolatry (v. 23) and immorality (vv. 26-27), characteristic practices of pagan behavior.

Hard on the heels of the idea that the righteousness of God is revealed in the gospel (v.17), Paul adds in the very next verse that the wrath of God is also revealed against ungodliness and wickedness. "Wrath" is a term that often makes us uncomfortable for we often picture it as the opposite of love. How could a God of love also be a God of wrath? Our problem probably stems from our equating divine wrath with human anger that tends to be capricious, irrational, arbitrary, biased, and inequitable. How could this emotional response be characteristic of God? For Paul, it is not. Divine wrath, rather, is the reaction of one who is totally good to anything that is evil, the recoiling of God from anything that contaminates or corrupts the goodness God intended in the created order.

Wrath and righteousness are dual activities of God. They are like two sides of the same coin. The righteousness of God is revealed in the gospel for the one who responds in faith to God. Wrath is revealed for the one who rejects. Not to choose one is to choose the other.

Have the Gentiles consciously rejected God? Since they have not received the self-disclosure God has given to Israel, should they be subject to God's wrath? Paul's answer is yes. But how could they reject what they have not known? Echoing the Psalmist who declared, "The heavens are telling the glory of God; and the firmament proclaims his handiwork" (Ps 19:1), Paul affirms that from the beginning of creation God's divinity and power have been disclosed in everything he has made (Rom 1:20). The human problem is not the lack of divine revelation, but the failure to respond positively to it. Instead of worshiping the creator, humankind worshiped the things that were created (v. 23). Although Paul is apparently describing the Gentiles in this passage, we should not forget Israel's own flirtations with idolatry. What he has said about the Gentiles is therefore applicable also to the Jews; Paul's point is the universal sinfulness of humankind.

As a result of this rejection of God, God gave humankind up (1:24, 26, 28). Note, the text does not say that God gave up on them, but that he gave them up to impurity (1:24), to degrading passions (1:26), and to a debased mind and things that should not be done (1:28). In other words, God gave them up to themselves, to suffer the consequences of their actions. Do not psychologists suggest that the best discipline for teaching children is to impose punishments that involve suffering the consequences of what they have done? This is precisely the action taken by God with sinful human beings both then and now: God allows us to suffer the consequences of our actions. An old proverb states the idea this way: "You've made your bed; now lie in it." In part this is Paul's own affirmation: "You reap whatever you sow" (Gal 6:7).

Paul paints a bleak picture of the predicament of the Gentiles. They have rejected the Creator in favor of the creature, and they are suffering the dire consequences of being given up to themselves. They are in desperate need of a new standing before God.

Lest the Jews become smug about the plight of the Gentiles, Paul then turns to them in 2:1. Here Paul employs the rhetorical device of diatribe, a style of writing in which the author carries on a conversation or debate with an imagined opponent.[4] Although the term "Jew" is not used until verse 17, the entire passage is directed to the Jew who assumes an inherent superiority to Gentiles because of possessing the Law (2:17-24) and practicing circumcision (2:25-29). Paul suggests that his opponent hears the Law but does not act in accordance with it (2:13), teaches the Law but does not obey it (2:21-23). In fact, some Gentiles who are ignorant of the

Law but who instinctively do what the Law requires will fare better at the time of judgment than the Jew who has known but disobeyed the Law (2:14-16). Doing, not just hearing, the Law is what is required (2:13). Circumcision, further, in and of itself is useless. For the Jew, this physical mark symbolized membership in the covenant community bound by the Law. Failure to observe the Law, though, nullifies the meaning of circumcision (v. 25). True circumcision, that which identifies a person as one who belongs to God, is not external or physical; it is internal, or a matter of the heart (2:28-29). Consequently, the true Jew is not one who bases his standing before God on externals, but one who is a Jew inwardly.

Paul's picture of the Jews is as bleak as that of the Gentiles. Even though they have enjoyed the privilege of God's special revelation through the Law, they have failed to live by it. They, too, are in need of a new standing before God.

Paul summarizes his argument in 3:9-20. Jews and Gentiles alike have failed. They are all under the power of sin, that sinister force that has engulfed the whole human race. Everyone is in need of the righteousness that comes through faith. Humankind is like a book on a shelf that has fallen over; nothing it can do will make it upright again. Only a force outside itself can make it right.

The Divine Solution

Just as the predicament of human beings is universal, so also is the solution. God's righteousness, the activity of making people right, has now become a reality through Jesus Christ for all who have faith (3:21-22). Just as all, Jew and Gentile alike, have sinned (3:23), now salvation is available for all who believe. That which human beings could not do for themselves God has provided.

The salvific act of God in Christ is the stackpole of Christian faith. Indeed much of the New Testament is devoted not only to the fact of what God has done but also to various attempts to explain the essence of this action and its results. None of these explanations alone fully captures the meaning of salvation. Perhaps this is why Paul uses three different metaphors within the scope of two verses to suggest what God has accomplished in Christ (3:24-25).

The first is justification. As we have seen, the root meaning of this word deals with making something right; but we cannot overlook the fact that in time the term also took on legal connotations. Because of his linking of the word here with other descriptive analogies, perhaps that is the idea Paul has in mind here. He has just described the Jews as Law breakers—those who had failed to meet all of the Law's requirements. What better way to speak to those who have experienced failure regarding the Law than by an image connoting restoration to right standing in a court of law!

For a second word picture of salvation Paul uses the idea of redemption. Other than in the language of the church, our use of this term is practically limited to store coupons—we redeem them for cash. In the first century, however, redemption connoted payment of the purchase price of a slave in order to set the slave free. In a world where slavery was an accepted fact of everyday life and in which slaves formed a sizable portion of the population, what better way to describe salvation than emancipation from the enslavement to sin! As Paul aptly proclaims in Galatians 5:1: "For freedom Christ has set us free!"

Finally, in this series of images Paul mentions an analogy from worship that focuses on animal sacrifice. English versions differ in their translations of the Greek word here. The King James Version uses "propitiation," a term drawn from pagan sacrificial systems in which the sacrifice was offered to appease a deity. Propitiation is not an action of the deity; instead, the deity is the recipient of the action. An animal is sacrificed in order that the deity will be placated. In the Revised English Bible the translation suggests "expiation," an action in which God is the subject and sin is the object. In this activity God blots out or obliterates sin. A third option is the "place where atonement occurs" or, by extension, "the sacrifice of atonement." This idea is preferred in the New Revised Standard Version. Either of the last two translations comes closer to what I think Paul has in mind, for both imply an activity of God in which the sinner is forgiven. Just as Paul sees justification, making right, as an action in which God is the subject, likewise he asserts the same kind of idea here.

As he has associated righteousness with the idea of faith in 1:16-17, Paul again emphasizes the role of faith in this act of salvation. He is the God of both Jew and Gentile who justifies both on the basis of faith (3:29-30).

Returning to the diatribe style in chapter 4, Paul again answers an imaginary Jewish opponent. Anticipating an argument about Abraham whom the Jews considered justified on the basis of works, Paul responds by quoting Genesis 15:6: "Abraham believed God, and it was reckoned to him as righteousness" (4:3). Remember that "believe" = "have faith in," and "righteousness" = "justification." Abraham, too, was justified by faith; this action was God's gift (grace) and not something Abraham earned. Circumcision, for example, was not an act that merited this status before God, for God deemed Abraham righteous before he was circumcised (4:10).

Moreover, Abraham was not justified on the basis of the Law (4:13), for he lived many generations before the Law was given at Sinai. For Paul, Abraham is the great example of justification by faith. Just as his faith was "reckoned to him as righteousness," so also is the case for everyone who believes (has faith) in the one who raised Jesus from the dead (4:24). Abraham is the spiritual father of all who believe, whether circumcised or not, whether Jew or Gentile (4:11b, 16, 23-25). Here, then, is Paul's theological foundation for the mission to the Gentiles: all who respond in faith to God are justified, whether Jew or Greek. Physical descent from Abraham, a source of pride for the Jews, is irrelevant: anyone who responds to God in faith can claim Abraham as father.[5]

To the problem of universal sinfulness, God has provided a solution. By the grace of God, right standing before God is available through faith in Jesus Christ for everyone who believes (4:22).

The Consequences of Salvation

After describing the plight of humankind and the gracious provision of God, Paul then describes in chapters 5–8 the results of this righteousness based on faith. First, he expounds upon the effects of salvation by developing another metaphor: reconciliation. The other terms he has used—justification, redemption, and expiation (atoning sacrifice)—do not have the same impact for us as they did for first-century readers, because we basically do not see ourselves as lawbreakers or slaves, and we are far removed from the idea of ritual sacrifice. We can easily resonate, however, with the idea of reconciliation. Alienation, the opposite of reconciliation, permeates our society in the breakdown of relationships between individuals, races, generations, genders, social classes, and nations. Hostility between individuals and between groups is a part of modern existence. Thus we quickly identify with Paul's description of the plight of sinful humanity as alienation from God. Further, we realize that we are powerless to break down this barrier between God and humanity. We relate to Paul's understanding of reconciliation: God has taken the initiative, reconciling us to Himself through the death of His Son (Rom 5:10-11; 2 Cor 5:18-21).[6] The result of this reconciliation is freedom from estrangement and peace with God (Rom 5:1).

How can the act of one man, the death of Jesus on the cross, affect so many others? Paul finds an analogy in the experience of another Old Testament character, Adam. Just as the disobedience of the one man Adam resulted in the entry of sin and death into the world (5:12, 17), so also the obedience of the one man Jesus Christ has resulted in grace and right standing before God (5:15-17). Even as the sin of Adam led to condemnation for all, so the action of Jesus leads to life for all (5:18). Christ has reversed the sin of Adam!

Consequently, those who have experienced the righteousness that comes through faith in Jesus Christ have also experienced freedom from the dominion of sin. This reality Paul demonstrates by drawing two analogies. First, Christian baptism depicts the identification of the believer with the

experience of Jesus. Just as Jesus died to sin, once for all
(6:10), so we, too, have died to sin and are free from enslavement to it (6:2, 6-7). Sin has lost its stranglehold on us. When
we are buried in the baptismal waters, we symbolically reen-
act Jesus' experience of death to sin. Baptism reflects the
death and burial of our old self that was alienated from God.
But it also depicts our rising with Christ to a new life, free
from sin's enslavement. Certainly Paul does not mean that
after baptism we will not commit individual sins, as his
admonitions in 6:12-13 indicate. Rather, because of the
accomplishment of Christ, the believer is no longer
dominated by sin (6:14).

At this point we should pause to remember the nature of
Paul's theological discussion. Although Romans presents an
orderly account of his understanding of the gospel, he is not
trying to present here all his thoughts on every theological
subject. For example, he talks about death to sin as a consequence of salvation, as a remedy to the plight he described in
Romans 1–2. As he mentions emulating Jesus' death in the
rite of baptism, he of consequence also mentions resurrection
(6:5), indicating that we will be raised like he was. His
emphasis, though, is not upon resurrection but upon the
defeat of sin, the solution to the plight of humankind. To see
his thoughts on resurrection, one must look to other texts
whose occasion gives rise to a discussion of the significance
of this event. In 1 Corinthians 15 resurrection dominates his
discussion because he writes to people who are denying its
reality (1 Cor 15:12).

Paul's second analogy that illustrates freedom from sin is
that of slavery (Rom 6:15-23). Earlier Paul has used redemption, the emancipation from slavery, as a metaphor of
salvation (3:24); but at the beginning of the letter he identified himself as a slave of Christ (1:1). His analogy in Romans
6 is consistent with his earlier allusions: the believer was
once enslaved to sin but now is enslaved to Christ. The purchase price has been paid, and the believer has been bought
by a new master (6:18, 22). Consequently, sin can no longer
dominate the believer's life.

The believer, then, is free from estrangement from God and free from sin's domination. But there is also a third area in which the believer finds liberty, or freedom from the Law (7:1-25). In an earlier letter, Galatians, Paul expounded at great length upon this theme. There the occasion was the heretical teaching that faith in Christ was not sufficient for salvation, that Gentile believers were obligated to obey the Mosaic Law in order to be Christians. Here in Romans Paul deals with the issue in more summary fashion: the Law is another entity from which the believer has been set free. To illustrate his point, Paul again utilizes a word picture, this time marriage (7:1-6). Apparently, his point is that just as a marriage relationship is nullified by the death of one of the two spouses, so the Christian who was formerly married to the Law has died and is now free to marry another, Christ (7:4).

Paul's attitude toward the Law has sparked much scholarly debate. At times he speaks positively about it (Rom 3:31; 7:12); other times he insists on its inadequacies (3:20; 4:15; 5:20; 7:7-11). Without becoming bogged down in the various options I have presented, let me suggest that for Paul, the Law is of divine origin but also partial and incomplete in comparison with the final and complete revelation that has come through Jesus Christ (8:3). In the matter of salvation, therefore, the regulations it demands, what Paul often calls the works of the Law, are inadequate substitutes for the grace of God that has been demonstrated in the death/resurrection of Jesus. The believer is free from the Law.

Paul concludes his discussion of the consequences of salvation by emphasizing the believer's life in the Spirit (8:1-39). In chapters 1–7 Paul mentions "spirit" five times; in chapters 9–16 he uses the word eight more times. In chapter 8, however, the word is found twenty-one times; this is Paul's most extensive discussion of the Spirit. In one breath Paul talks about the believer's being in the Spirit and the Spirit's being in the believer (8:9), just as he talks about the believer's being in Christ (8:1) and Christ's being in the believer (8:10). Paul is not describing different experiences or realities, for "the

Lord is the Spirit" (2 Cor 3:17). In fact, if one does not have the Spirit of Christ, she or he does not belong to him (Rom 8:9). The Spirit has set us free from sin and death (8:2); the Spirit assures us of our status as God's children (8:16); and the Spirit intercedes on our behalf (8:27). Because of this relationship, absolutely nothing can separate us from the love of God in Christ Jesus (8:39)

Again, Paul has not outlined in this letter all his beliefs. Other important reflections, for example, about his understanding of Christ (Christology), the church (ecclesiology), and the return of Christ (eschatology) are scattered among the other epistles as those ideas fit the occasion he is addressing. For the essence of his thought, though, nothing compares to this first half of Romans where he explores the response of the God of grace to human need and the consequences of that response for the believer.

Notes

[1]The letter also includes Paul's advice about some ethical matters, which we will examine in the next chapter.

[2]Other Pauline texts where this phrase is found include: Rom 3:26; Gal 2:26; 3:22. Variations that have the title Christ without the name Jesus are Gal 2:16; Phil 3:9. Passages that have "through faith" or "by faith" without mentioning Jesus (Christ) are Rom 3:25, 28; 5:1; Gal 3:8, 11, 14, 24, 26; 5:5.

[3]Gal 3:26; Col 1:4; 2:5; 2 Tim 3:15. See especially Gal 2:16 where Paul has two of the ambiguous "faith of/in Jesus" statements, separated by the explicit statement using the preposition "we have believed *in* Christ Jesus." It seems that the middle phrase explains the other two. Also see Rom 4:24 where Paul mentions "we who believe (have faith) in him who raised Jesus. . . ."

[4]In the diatribe, when Paul verbalizes as direct quotations the objections of his imaginary opponents, many modern translations print these responses of the opponent in quotation marks. See, for example, 1 Cor 6:12-13; 7:1. This feature is helpful in interpretation for it shows that Paul is quoting his opponents and not stating his own views.

[5]See Paul's similar argument in Gal 4:21–5:1.

[6]See also Eph 2:13-22; Col 1:19-23.

Paul, the Pastor

Paul's writings impart the reasoned conclusions of a theologian reflecting on the significance of the Christ event. As we have seen, though, Paul functions as a theologian from a pastoral perspective. He does not formulate a systematic theology. Rather, for the most part, his theological reflections are recorded in response to particular questions or doctrinal interests of the churches he has left behind. His letters disclose the heart of a loving pastor concerned about the daily lives of those whom he has brought to Christ. Those concerns, though, are not limited to doctrinal issues; they are also related to matters of proper behavior. Ethics, as well as theology, is constitutive of Paul's thought.

For Paul, belief and behavior go hand in hand. A person cannot have one without the other. What one believes affects how he or she lives. The Christian life is practical rather than theoretical. Evidence that one is rightly related to God is not found in a list of doctrines one professes as much as it is in the way the person lives.

Therefore, we should not be surprised to find a heavy emphasis on ethical matters in Paul's writings. At times the ethical material is scattered throughout a letter, virtually intertwined with theological matter. First Corinthians is a good example. At other times, after a lengthy theological exposition, Paul turns to the ethical materials with a "therefore." Some wag has said that when one finds a "therefore" in a text, he or she ought to see what it is there for. When Paul uses the term, he is deliberate, saying that the ethical advice that follows is based on the theological assumptions he has just proposed: because these things are true, then act in this way. Examples include Romans 12:1 and Ephesians 4:1.

Sometimes the ethical admonitions are of a general nature; though directed to a particular church, they deal with practical issues applicable to all Christians in all churches. Romans 12:9-21 is comprised of a list of such teachings. At other times Paul's ethical advice is very pointed, dealing with a particular situation in a particular church at a particular time. In 1 Corinthians 5:1-8, for example, Paul addresses a problem of incest within the church at Corinth.

Undoubtedly, some ethical admonitions of Paul reflect the accepted customs of his day, and they seem to have little relevance for the present. Of such are the instructions to the Corinthians about proper hairstyles: men should not have long hair, but women should (1 Cor 11:14-15)! Other advice is timeless, applicable to Christians today as much as it was to the first-century readers. Again Romans 12:9-21 is illustrative of this type of material.[1]

Sometimes Paul's advice is sought by the church to which he is writing. The Corinthians obviously sent a letter with questions about several matters to which Paul responds (1 Cor 7:1). At other times Paul writes unsolicited advice concerning problems about which he has heard. As we have seen, Paul did not found or visit the church at Rome; yet he writes to them about a divisive problem within their community (Rom 14:1–15:13). Since God called him to be a minister to the Gentiles, and since the Roman church is predominantly Gentile, he feels it appropriate for him to write to them a word of "reminder" (15:15).

Whether general or specific, whether solicited or not, the ethical instructions Paul includes in his letters are given from a pastoral perspective.[2] Paul does not formulate an ethical system any more than he does a theological one; he does not have an outline of Christian ethics any more than he has one of Christian theology. His responses are suited to a particular occasion. Thus he does not attempt to deal theoretically with every possible issue that might arise. Neither does he make up lists of rules and regulations to be imposed on a community. Instead, he deals with very real issues for very real readers, giving concrete examples of behavior that is consistent with Christian belief. In this advice he gives, although he does not have a list of rules, he appears to have some guiding principles that shape his thought; these are the starting points for the specific instructions he gives to his readers.

Love

In the orderly presentation of Paul's theological perspective found in Romans 1–8, the climactic statement concerns God's love (8:35-39). "Nothing," exclaims Paul, "can separate us from it!" For Paul, it was the love of God that sought the solution to the problem caused by humanity's sin. We were alienated from God and unable on our own to bridge the gap that separated us from him. God, though, did what we could not do. God demonstrated for us in the action of Christ in that "while we were still sinners Christ died for us" (Rom 5:8; Eph 2:4). Certainly at the core of his understanding of the Deity is the concept of God's love.

Paul characterizes the basic human response to God as faith, the openness to receive what God has offered. Because of what God has done for us and because of our response in faith to God, Paul then calls on us not to be conformed to the standards of this world (Rom 12:2), but to be conformed to the image of Christ (8:29), the one who loved us and gave himself for us (Eph 5:2). Does not conformity to Christ imply a conformity to a self-giving love like his? It comes as no surprise, therefore, to find that at the heart of Paul's understanding of how the Christian is to live is the concept of love. Love not only stands at the center of his theology, but also it is the cardinal principle that shapes his ethical thought.

Actually, when Paul discusses love as a characteristic of the believer, he says little about the love of the believer for God (1 Cor 16:22; 2 Cor 2:8). That, I think, is basically understood. Rather, his statements about love flow out of his understanding of conforming to Christ; thus his emphasis is upon loving others with a volitional love that is self-giving, seeking the best for others rather than for the self. The idea comes across in his choice of words. Typically, when Paul talks about the love God has for people, he uses the Greek word *agape*, a term that describes this selfless type of love. In turn, that divine type of love is what he expects believers to emulate. No finer statement of his understanding of this kind of love can be found than that in 1 Corinthians 13. This love is patient and kind; it is not envious, arrogant, boastful, or rude; it does not insist on its own way (vv. 4-5). In fact, faith without this kind of love is worthless (v. 2); "the only thing that counts is faith working through love" (Gal 5:6).[3]

So significant is love for Paul, furthermore, that he repeatedly insists that the Law is summed up in the commandment to love neighbor as self (Gal 5:14; Rom 13:8-10). Paul evidently saw some elements of the Law as nullified by the coming of Christ, particularly those ritual requirements such as circumcision and food laws that erected barriers between Jews and Gentiles. The moral law, though, he saw as binding; and he saw that it was fulfilled in love.

When Paul lists the fruit of the Spirit, love is placed first (Gal 5:22). When Paul discusses spiritual gifts (1 Cor 12–14), he encourages the readers to strive for the greater gifts, indicating he will show them "a still more excellent way" (v. 31). That more excellent way is love (1 Cor 13). Without love, the other spiritual gifts are meaningless (vv. 1-3). Repeatedly, then, Paul reminds his readers to love (Rom 12:9-10; 1 Cor 14:1; 16:14; 2 Cor 6:6; Gal 5:13; Eph 4:2; Phil 1:9; 2:2; Col 2:2; 3:14; 1 Thess 3:12; 4:9-10).

Years ago I saw a poster that proclaimed: "Love is something you do." These words, I feel, express Paul's understanding. Two incidents in particular come to mind. In Chapter 5 we looked at the collection ministry of Paul, noting the practical and theological significance of this venture by which Paul hoped to bridge the gap between Jewish and Gentile Christianity in the first century. Especially interesting in this context are the words of encouragement Paul gave to the Corinthians to motivate their participation. Mentioning the generosity of the Macedonian churches in spite of their own economic hardship (2 Cor 8:1-6), Paul calls on the Corinthians to excel in this undertaking as they do in "everything" (v. 7). Although his request is not in the form of a command, Paul suggests that their participation in the collection is a demonstration and proof of the genuineness of their love (vv. 8, 24). For Paul, love is not simply an emotion, nor is it a mere platitude. Love is demonstrated in action—in this case, sharing financially with the Jewish Christians who are in need.

Second, in Romans Paul gives another specific example of love in action. Although the ethical advice Paul has shared in Romans 12–13 is of a general type that could easily apply to any first-century Christian reader, in Romans 14 he deals with a particular problem confronting this church: a tension between the "strong" and the "weak." Paul does not specifically identify either of the two groups, but scholars, on the one hand, generally associate the "weak" with Jewish Christians who had scruples about dietary practices (14:2, 21) and the proper day for worship (14:5-6). The "strong," on the other hand, were probably Gentile Christians who did not feel the strictures of regulations about unclean foods and Sabbath rules. This latter group was evidently in the majority, and Paul's admonitions were directed primarily, though not exclusively, to them (15:1). He encourages each of them to accept the other (14:1; 15:7), and he insists that neither pass judgment on the other (14:3, 13). Further, he pointedly instructs the strong not to violate the scruples of the weak by insisting on practicing the freedoms they feel have been granted to them by Christ (vv. 13-23).

The teaching here is similar to the problem of meat sacrificed to idols Paul addresses in 1 Corinthians 8. The principle there is the same he stresses here: Christians should not use their freedom at the expense of their weaker brothers and sisters (Rom 14:20-23; 1 Cor 8:9-13). Paul's sense of freedom included the right to refrain from exercising it, if his freedom caused others to stumble. For Paul, when the strong insisted on their rights to the detriment of those about them, they were "no longer walking in love" (Rom 14:15). Love, not freedom, is the key to Christian behavior.

The Body of Christ

A second guiding principle for Paul is the recognition of the church as the body of Christ. Fully developed in 1 Corinthians 12, Paul's metaphor of the "one body" is also found in 1 Corinthians 10:17 and Romans 12:4-5; and allusions to it occur in Ephesians 1:23 and 4:2, 4, 16 and in Colossians 1:18, 24 and 2:19 and 3:15. By this figure of speech Paul stresses both the unity and diversity found within the church. Unity characterizes not only the relationship of the believer with Christ, but also the relationship with other Christians. Whatever affects one part of the body affects the body as a whole; whatever affects a part of the body affects Christ also. Remember the heavenly voice of Christ speaking to Paul on the way to Damascus to destroy the church there: "Saul, Saul, why do you persecute me?" (Acts 9:4). Diversity is found in the function of the different members, compared by Paul to parts of the human body. Just as the foot, hand, ear, and eye have distinctive tasks (1 Cor 12:16-26), so individual Christians have different functions in the church (vv. 6-11). In both bodies—the human and the church—individual members exist and function not for the sake of that individual, but for the sake of the body as a whole. The eye, for example, does not see just for the eye, but also for the ear, foot, hand, and the rest of the body. The diversity of functions actually strengthens the body.

Unity of and within the body of Christ, then, was of paramount importance to Paul. Paul went to the Jerusalem Conference to preserve the oneness of the church. The desire to heal division and restore unity motivated him to take up the collection. This desire for unity also served as the catalyst calling forth much of Paul's ethical instruction, for internal division and dissension plagued the church of the first century. In the church at Corinth alone, for example, groups asserting loyalty to different church leaders were decimating the harmony of the congregation (1 Cor 1:10-17; 3:1-23); divisive factions, perhaps along social class lines, were destroying the significance of the Lord's Supper by their fractious observance of the rite (11:17-33); and misunderstandings about the nature of spiritual gifts were driving wedges between fellow Christians. In Corinth and Rome alike there were unity-threatening disputes about which foods should or should not be eaten. Moreover, the Philippian church was evidently struggling with some type of disagreement or divisiveness within the community. The cause for the dissension is not spelled out in Paul's reply, but it was evidently pervasive. Even church members who earlier had worked side by side with Paul were affected (Phil 4:2).

The response of Paul to the Philippians is illustrative of the kind of ethical advice he gave in these divisive situations. Paul repeatedly urges the Philippians to be of one mind (Phil 1:27; 2:2; 3:15), not looking out for their own interests but for the interests of others (2:4). Interesting here is his quotation of a christological hymn that describes Christ as an example of one who did not assert his own self-interest (2:5-11). Finally, he implores Euodia and Syntyche, the two women who had labored with him, to resolve their differences (4:2). Paul writes as a pastor concerned about the divisiveness that has permeated the Philippian community. His call for harmony is personal; individuals for whom he has great affection are involved. His call is also theological, for it is derived from his basic belief about the unity of the church, the body of Christ.[4]

Note that these two themes of love and the body of Christ are intertwined. Paul advocated the collection because of his beliefs about both love and unity within the body of Christ. The advice he gave in response to the problem of the strong and the weak was evoked by the same two beliefs. The instructions to the Corinthians and the Philippians about their divisions were elicited not only by Paul's beliefs about the body, but also because of his belief that they should do everything in love (1 Cor 16:14; Phil 2:2). For Paul, belief demanded a certain behavior!

The Example of Christ

Before leaving these general themes that undergird Paul's ethics, one factor that evidently shaped his thinking remains. Paul's responses to particular problems were also based on his understanding that the believer should imitate Christ. This idea was first suggested to me several months ago when I reread A. M. Hunter's little introduction to Paul,[5] but I did not think much of the idea, especially since Hunter cited only three verses to support his point. Putting Hunter aside, I became involved in the study of Acts and of the life of Paul. When I decided to devote one chapter in this present work to the ethics of Paul, I concluded that I would cite examples of the general principles that I feel provided the foundation for Paul's thought. Imagine my surprise, then, when I suddenly realized that the texts I selected contained those verses that Hunter had cited so long ago. I have concluded that he was right: for Paul, the example of Christ was foundational for Christian ethics.

Do you remember the century-old little Christian classic entitled *In His Steps*? In this fictional account by Charles M. Sheldon the central character asks himself daily as he is confronted with every new situation and challenge, "What would Jesus do in this set of circumstances?" Frankly, accepting the idea that Jesus is the sinless Son of God, we would have to admit that it is impossible for us, sinners that we are, to imitate Jesus in every situation or always to do precisely what he would do. There is hardly a one of us, though, who at some time has not asked herself or himself this question in a difficult spot in order to determine the right thing to do. Now, it is true that Paul does not verbalize the question, "What would Jesus do?" In three significant texts, though, he does hold Christ up as an example to be emulated.

In confronting the strong and the weak in the Roman church, Paul insists that instead of letting their differences drive a wedge between them, they should accept one another (Rom 15:7). Motivation for this action is found in the experience of Jesus: just as he has accepted both strong and weak, so also should the Roman Christians welcome each other. In

fact, Christ is the perfect example of one who did not set out
to please himself (v. 3), acting only in accord with his own
self-interests. Just as he forgot self in order to serve the needs
of others, so should the strong put aside their concerns and
put up with the failures of the weak in order to build them up
(vv. 1-2).

Similar to this admonition are Paul's words introducing
the great hymn to Christ in Philippians 2:5-11. Remember
that the Philippians were at odds with one another, and their
divisiveness was threatening their community life. Paul's
advice to them was: "Do nothing from selfish ambition or
conceit, but in humility regard others as better than your-
selves. Let each of you look not to your own interests, but to
the interests of others" (vv. 3-4). To illustrate the point of his
advice, then, Paul cited the hymn whose opening lines stress
the humility of Jesus. This humility, Paul said, should be a
model for them to imitate (v. 5).

Paul also encourages the Corinthians to emulate Christ.
Writing about the collection, and encouraging the readers to
excel in their giving, Paul reminds them of the generosity of
Jesus Christ who, though he was rich, became poor for their
sakes (2 Cor 8:9). As Christ was generous to others, so should
they be to those in Jerusalem.

The imitation of Christ motif in Paul is further supported,
ironically, in two letters where Paul admonishes the readers
to imitate *Paul* (Phil 3:17; 4:9; 1 Cor 11:1). When I first
started a serious study of Paul in seminary, these verses both-
ered me. I saw Paul as quintessentially egotistical. The more I
studied, though, the more I became convinced that my initial
impression had been wrong. In both instances Paul was writing to Christian communities he had founded, to people who
knew him well. As a matter of fact, these communities were
composed of new Christians, none of whom had been a Christian longer than Paul. He was the most seasoned Christian
they knew. Thus, if they were to look to anyone as an example, Paul was the most likely candidate. Rather than asserting
his own ego, by including these admonitions, Paul was actually challenging himself to live a circumspect life. Paul felt a

responsibility to these people to be the best example he could be, for they had no others. This feeling I think is expressed in the Corinthians letter:

> So, . . . whatever you do, do everything for the glory of God. Give no offense to Jews or to Greeks or to the church of God, just as I try to please everyone in everything I do, not seeking my own advantage, but that of many, so that they may be saved. Be imitators of me, as I am of Christ. (1 Cor 10:31–11:1)

The imitation of Christ was a goal for Paul; he advised his readers to set the same standard for themselves. In his three examples of imitating Christ we should note that the readers were not so much called to mimic Christ's actions as they were to emulate Christ's attitudes: an inclusiveness that accepted everyone, a humility that sacrificed the self for the sake of others, and a generosity that knew no bounds.

Conclusion

The letters of Paul disclose the innermost thoughts of a pioneer missionary and champion of the Christian faith, an apostle and theologian. They also reveal that this one had the heart of a pastor, a shepherd, deeply concerned about the day-to-day problems that confronted his flock. Thus, in addition to the lofty theology found within them, the letters also overflow with practical advice Paul gave to his readers about daily Christian living. In the representative texts we have examined that offer this apostolic counsel, three ideas are intertwined: the imitation of Christlike attitudes, the necessity for unity in the body of Christ, and the centrality of *agape*. These formed the foundation for Paul's ethics. Whether general or specific, whether requested or unsolicited, his practical advice was derived from these principles. Paul practiced what he preached These foundational ideas were not simply suggestions for his readers; they were the principles that guided his own daily living as he undertook his mission to the Gentiles.

Notes

[1]For an excellent presentation of Pauline ethical concerns, see Victor Paul Furnish, *The Moral Teaching of Paul: Selected Issues*, 2d ed., rev. (Nashville: Abingdon, 1985). Furnish insists upon interpreting these moral teachings in the light of Paul's cultural setting; he warns about treating these teachings as a "white elephant" or as a "sacred cow."

[2]J. Stanley Glen, *Pastoral Problems in First Corinthians* (Philadelphia: Westminster, 1964), discusses the ethical issues raised in this letter from a pastoral perspective.

[3]Paul frequently associates faith in Christ with love for others. See 1 Thess 3:6; 2 Thess 1:3; Phlm 1:5; Eph 1:15; 3:17; 6:23; Col 1:4. Please note that I have included references to 2 Thessalonians, Ephesians, and Colossians, letters that many consider *Deuteropauline* (written in Paul's name by close associates). Even if it could be proven that any one of these letters was not actually written by Paul, I would assert that it was written to express the essence of Paul's thought. Thus, with some caution we can find in these letters glimpses of Pauline theology.

[4]To understand the theme of unity in Paul's theology of the church, see also Ephesians, esp. 2:11-22 and 4:1-6.

[5]Archibald M. Hunter, *The Gospel According to St Paul* (Philadelphia: Westminster, 1966) esp. 45-46.

Afterword

The church's mission to the Gentiles dominates the New Testament. In addition to the narrative account contained in the New Testament's longest document, the 13 letters bearing Paul's name are byproducts of that mission. By count, then, 14 of the New Testament's 27 documents are related to this theme. By size, approximately 40 percent of the total New Testament is devoted to this enterprise.

Furthermore, the church's mission to the Gentiles dominated first-century Christian history. The story of the spread of the gospel from Jerusalem through Judea and Samaria to the uttermost parts of the earth, in fact, *is* the history of the first-century church. Apart from this phenomenal undertaking initiated by the Hellenists and brought to fruition by Paul, there is little else to tell about this period in the life of the post-resurrection community.

The church's mission to the Gentiles dominates the Christian faith to this day. It has shaped forever the nature of the church. It is our heritage. Since that first-century initiative, it has never ceased being the central task of the Christian community. For two thousand years the church has been devoted to the task of taking the gospel to the Gentiles. It is still our goal. Until everyone has heard the church's message, until the barriers that alienate people from each other—that separate Jew and Gentile, slave and free, male and female—are finally broken down, the community of faith will ever be engaged in the church's mission to the Gentiles.

For Further Reading

Brown, Raymond E. *An Introduction to the New Testament.* The Anchor Bible Reference Library. New York: Doubleday, 1997.

Bruce, F. F. *Peter, Stephen, James, and John: Studies in Early Non-Pauline Christianity.* Grand Rapids: Eerdmans, 1980.

Furnish, Victor Paul. *The Moral Teaching of Paul: Selected Issues,* 2d ed. rev. Nashville: Abingdon, 1985.

Harrisville, Roy A. *Romans.* Augsburg Commentary on the New Testament. Minneapolis: Augsburg, 1980.

Hunter, Archibald M. *The Gospel According to St Paul.* Philadelphia: Westminster, 1966.

Jewett, Robert. *A Chronology of Paul's Life.* Philadelphia: Fortress, 1979.

Johnson, Sherman E. *Paul the Apostle and His Cities.* Good News Studies 21. Wilmington DE: Michael Glazier, 1987.

Keck, Leander. *Paul and His Letters.* Proclamation Commentaries: The New Testament Witnesses for Preaching. Philadelphia: Fortress, 1979.

Knox, John. *Chapters in the Life of Paul,* rev. ed. Macon GA: Mercer University Press, 1987.

Krodel, Gerhard. *Acts*. Proclamation Commentaries: The New Testament Witnesses for Preaching. Philadelphia: Fortress, 1981.

Parsons, Mikeal C. "Acts of the Apostles," in *Mercer Commentary on the Bible*. Macon GA: Mercer University Press, 1995.

Polhill, John B. *Acts*. The New American Commentary, Vol. 26. Nashville: Broadman, 1992.

Stagg, Frank. *The Book of Acts: The Early Struggle for an Unhindered Gospel*. Nashville: Braodman, 1955.

ALL THE BIBLE

ALL THE BIBLE SERIES DESCRIPTION

AREA	TITLE*
Genesis–Deuteronomy	*Journey to the Land of Promise*
Former Prophets	*From Promise to Exile*
Latter Prophets, excluding Postexilic	*God's Servants, the Prophets*
Poetry, Wisdom Literature	*The Testimony of Poets and Sages*
Exilic, Postexilic Books	*The Exile and Beyond*
The Four Gospels	*The Church's Portraits of Jesus*
Acts of the Apostles, Epistles of Paul	*The Church's Mission to the Gentiles*
Hebrews–Revelation	*The Church as a Pilgrim People*

*subject to change